also by mark leyner

I Smell Esther Williams (1983)

My Cousin, My Gastroenterologist (1990)

Et Tu, Babe (1992)

tooth

imprints

on a

corn dog

mark leyner

harmony books • new york

The selections below first appeared in the following publications:
"Hulk Couture"—*Esquire Gentleman*
"Immoral Allure"—*Esquire Gentleman*
"The (Illustrated) Body Politic" (previously titled "Senate Tattoo")—
The New York Times Op-Ed
"Great Pretenders" (previously titled "Faux to Faux")—*The New Yorker*
"Dream Girls, USA" (previously titled "Miss America")—*Elle*
"Dangerous Dads"—*Esquire Gentleman*
"Eat at Cosmo's" (previously titled "Spook the Sponsors")—*The New Yorker*
"Oh, Brother" (previously titled "The Zeichner Twins")—*The New Republic*

Published by Harmony Books, a division of
Crown Publishers, Inc., 201 East 50th Street,
New York, New York 10022. Member of the
Crown Publishing Group.
Random House, Inc. New York, Toronto, London, Sydney, Auckland
HARMONY and colophon are trademarks of Crown Publishers, Inc.
Manufactured in the United States of America
Design by Debbie Glasserman

Library of Congress Cataloging-in-Publication Data

Leyner, Mark.
Tooth imprints on a corn dog / Mark Leyner.
p.   cm.
I. Title.
PS3562.E99T66   1995
813'.54—dc20
94-38570
CIP

ISBN 0-517-59384-X
10 9 8 7 6 5 4 3 2 1
First Edition

contents

tooth

imprints

on a

corn dog

When Merci was wheeled into the operating room to undergo the C-section that extricated our daughter, Gabrielle, from the umbilical knot she'd tied around her leg, the doctors set up this curtain that divided Merci into two sectors: the upper part for nonparticipants—Merci and me—and the business end, which apparently was for M.D.s and R.N.s only. Now, I *love* surgery—so as soon as I deduced that they were about to make the first incision, I got up and started to walk around to where the action was, because I couldn't see a damn thing up at Merci's head, and by this point she was sufficiently anesthetized and tranquilized that I figured she didn't need my "moral support" anymore, plus the fact that, in order to be allowed into the operating room, I'd scrubbed with hexachlorophene and donned full surgical regalia—gown, cap, mask, and gloves. Now, putting me in surgical garb is like putting a drag queen in an Yves Saint Laurent evening gown—I just light up. (Often I feel like a surgeon trapped in a writer's body.)

Anyway, as soon as the doctors see me coming, they get very peremptory and very territorial about Merci's uterus: "Mr. Leyner, please! You're to remain on that side of the curtain or you're going to have to wait outside."

Merci hears this, lifts her head up, and says in her sweet little voice, frayed only slightly by some 30 hours of labor: "Doctors, it's perfectly OK for him to assist—he watches a lot of medical programming on cable TV on Sundays."

The logic of this statement is so cogent and irrefutable that the doctors all just shrug their shoulders as if to say: "Well, that's about equivalent to the training we have, so welcome aboard, c'mon down, have a hemostat, grab a retractor, etc."

This incident exemplifies Merci—her sense of humor and sangfroid in the midst of difficult circumstances, her bracing pragmatism articulated in her dulcet Ecuadorian Tinker Bell voice. One of the coolest things about Merci is the way she talks. I need only slightly amend Michael Kimmelman's description of art historian Meyer Shapiro's writing to characterize Merci's discourse. Something like: "Her chirpy-timbred buoyant palaver, while uncompromising, dense, and dizzying in its references, is without cant or pomp."

People have said about me "unfettered imagination, nice arms," but she's got a pretty unfettered imagination herself. It's probably just as likely for her to say, just out of the blue, something like "bioluminescent acne" as it would be for me.

Don't you find it really revolting when an author thanks his wife by saying: "Only a woman with so-and-so's understanding and patience would have endured my manic highs and sloughs of despond, my chilly remoteness and insularity, and, alternately, my infantile need to be burped and changed, my obsessive philandering, my inexplicable need to fuck every woman in her step class, my having squandered her Christmas Club money on my methamphetamine habit, the Charivari sprees, the cognac binges with the inevitable vomiting and weeping, my paranoia, my hypochondria, my loss of interest in personal grooming and hygiene, and a recent compulsion to titillate myself by putting larvae in her food—all of which, rightly or wrongly, I felt was necessary to get through this long creative night. Her editorial acumen and rigor, her wise encouragement and enabling love, etc. etc."? This is your basic "I'm so complex and difficult, and my wife is so simple and forbearing" (a.k.a. "simpering imbecile puts up with anything overweening dickhead dishes out") formula.

Well, interestingly enough, a perfectly inverse equation underlies life at the Pinto-Leyner household. Merci is the complex one, and she's delightful to live with. (In an article for the Neapolitan textile-design fanzine *Bistecca,* I think I said that she had "close to optimal interpersonal ergonomics.") How easily one pictures her researching Montessori schools in an ecru mohair tank top and peppering her conversation with Vivienne Westwood this and Benazir Bhutto that. Y'know what I'm saying?

On the other hand, I'm simple, but extremely difficult to live with. And it's not like I'm racked with self-reproach about it either. I'm just the cream soda swilling, crotch scratching, irascible, coughing-up-indigestible-bits-of-grizzle-from-some-meat-on-a-stick, surly, greasy overalls-over-candy-colored-latex-minikimono (my work uniform when I'm in the throes of a novel or a play), don't-bother-me-till-halftime kind of guy that society has made me. So hey, what the fuck? I'm not apologizing for who I am. I'm just trying to say that Merci is more complex, OK?

I'll give you an example: the gullibility ruse. Merci will feign gullibility in order to reveal and then revel in my own misreading of her apprehension. It's the sort of "you must *really* be naive if you think I'm that naive" game that she plays with such cunning. Here are several examples of "fun facts" that I've casually purveyed, only to find out weeks, sometimes months, later that, notwithstanding her feigned credulity, Merci had immediately dismissed as patently erroneous:

• Stephen Foster, the American songwriter and composer responsible for such enduring favorites as "Oh! Susannah" and "Camptown Races," had jet black hair growing from one armpit and bright red hair growing from the other— a genetic anomaly that occurs in only one out of 5 million people.

• Neville Chamberlain, the British statesman whose controversial policy of appeasing Adolf Hitler resulted in the 1938 Munich pact, refused to keep his contact lenses in the customary plastic storage case, preferring instead two rain-filled hoofprints.

• In the future, supermarkets may be able to keep their produce sections so cold that temperatures will approach 700 nanokelvins, or somewhat less than one millionth of a degree above absolute zero—minus 459 degrees Fahrenheit. (At this temperature, atoms merge with each other to become what are known as Bose-Einstein condensates—a hypothetical superatomic state of matter that may never have existed anywhere before.)

• In recent laboratory experiments, McDonald's has produced brewed coffee that is 6,000 kelvins, or 10,300 degrees Fahrenheit—the approximate surface temperature of the sun.

• As a young man, while studying songwriting with Oscar Hammerstein II, Stephen Sondheim decapitated a defrocked priest who propositioned him in a men's room at a Manhattan furniture showroom. The headless torso remained ambulatory for some 15 seconds, tottering out of the lavatory and collapsing finally on a sectional sofa. Charges against Sondheim were never filed and he went on to become one of Broadway's most esteemed composers and lyricists.

• While candy-striping at a veteran's hospital in Akron, Ohio, 15-year-old Dorothy Hamill was caught putting objects in the rectums of anesthetized patients as they lay unconscious in postoperative recovery. (The impounded objects are now on display in a vitrine in the hospital's lobby.) Thanks to the intercession of her father, a Kiwanis officer and alderman, Hamill was allowed to quietly plead nolo contendere and avoid the publicity of a trial. Hamill's gold medal for figure skating in the 1976 Winter Olympics captivated the country and her perky, blunt-cut hairdo became the coif de jour in salons across America.

• Boxer Sonny Liston so despised the taste and smell of buckwheat groats that his trainer would have a kasha effigy of his opponent brought to his dressing room minutes before a fight.

• During the Cuban missile crisis, President Kennedy was so adamant that his advisors remain available at every moment that he ordered them to wear diapers so that they wouldn't need to go to the bathroom. When the fastidious Secretary of State Dean Rusk demurred, he was briefly jailed.

• Martin Van Buren, the eighth president of the United States, had no bones or cartilage in his face. As a result of this abnormality, his face had the consistency of soft clay. This meant that it would become misshapen if kissed too roughly or handled at all. Sheet marks would last until his face was smoothed. If he slept on one side all night, he would wake up with that side of his face completely flattened. A sculptor was retained by the White House to re-mold Van Buren's face every day. But despite the efforts of the facial sculptor, his physiognomy varied wildly from day to day, as evidenced by portraits that show him with a bulbous nose on one day and a long aquiline nose on another, with high cheek bones and glinting blue eyes on one and a sloping forehead and rheumy, protruding eyes under a single continuous brow on another.

As I complete this dedication, I can't help but think back to a time some seven years ago. It was only a few weeks after I'd met Merci. I was in a paramilitary writers' colony in Idaho. One day we were on a 50-kilometer march with full pack and "composition intervals"—we were required to compose a poem at 15 km, an essay or short story at 25 km, and a novel outline and first chapter at 40 km.

There I was at the first interval, and all I'd produced was:

The pilot of a skywriting plane
suffers a fatal cerebral hemorrhage.
The aircraft falls,
scoring the immaculate azure
with a valedictory parabola of Dickinsonian dashes.

I knew this wouldn't be enough to satisfy my commanding officer, a sadistic taskmaster who considered anything under four or five stanzas a personal insult. I doffed my helmet and looked at a photograph of Merci that I'd taped inside. And there—in the first of by now innumerable occasions on which mere reference to her visage would inflame my imagination—gripping my legal pad and pen tightly against the backwash from helicopter rotors, I scrawled the full work:

The pilot of a skywriting plane
suffers a fatal cerebral hemorrhage.
The aircraft falls,
scoring the immaculate azure
with a valedictory parabola of Dickinsonian dashes.

Meanwhile, at the bar of a posh restaurant in
    Brentwood,
three couples without dinner reservations
wait so long for a table
that the women experience
synchronization of their ovulatory cycles.

Me, I'm just another prematurely wizened
    geek-savant.
Plucking a tiny stringed instrument
made out of a ring binder and orthodontic rubber
    bands,

I lie in a bath of hairy milk
and sing my lonesome blues.

[The fourth stanza has been redacted
because it doesn't fall within the scope of this poem.
And the time of the gentleman has expired.]

And so, Merci, I dedicate this *Corn Dog,* this red, sweating
sausage sheathed in cornmeal batter and impaled on a
honed stick, and each *Tooth Imprint*—each incisal pit and
molar ridge—to you.

I know, sweetie, that you're not crazy about me taking
this benthic pied-à-terre/atelier eleven kilometers below
the surface of the Pacific Ocean in the Mariana Trench,
some 320 kilometers southeast of Guam. But it's the only
way I thought I'd be able to get enough peace and quiet
and enough distance from the whole New York *scene* to
be able to complete the next two books I'm under contract for.

The place is pretty swanky considering that it has to
withstand about 16,000 pounds per square inch of pressure. When I need to shop, I travel back and forth to the
supply ship on the surface in a brand-new 1996 ceramic-
hull one-man submersible with a silver-zinc fuel cell, joy-
stick navigation, voice- and video-transmitting fiber-optic
microcable, taupe leather interior, roof rack, 5-disc
carousel CD player, 150-watt Bose speakers. My only
complaint is that it's a bit sluggish. And when you're
down here eleven kilometers from the mother ship and
you realize that you're out of coffee filters or those fabric
softener dryer sheets—it's a long trip back up at five knots
max. But work is going extremely well. Do you remem-

to merci pinto leyner

ber reading my proposal for a book called *The Tetherballs of Bougainville*? Do you remember how enthusiastic I was because I thought that not only would it be the first novel to really capture the febrile excitement of international tetherball competition but also the first novel to analyze tetherball as a kind of deep metaphor for fin de siècle gender relations? Does any of this sound familiar? There's a character named Colonel Alebua, Bougainville's despotic junta leader, a wild aficionado of American pop culture who names his daughter Kojacqueline. Ring a bell? Well, anyway, the novel's coming along marvelously, I think. And as soon as it's done, I'm contemplating a book-length meditation on the Edgar Winter song "Frankenstein." I don't know of another instrumental that speaks more powerfully to that strain of the American male psyche which yearns to grossly transform one's own body, swagger down an illuminated runway in a slaughterhouse-turned-disco thronged with Dionysian suburban housewives ululating with libidinal excess, and then launch oneself on a hallucinogen-fueled, out-of-body ascent that culminates in an orgasmic merge with a creature who manifests all the faces of the Dionysian housewives, but is in reality the huge throbbing cosmogonic placenta that was expelled nanoseconds after the birth of the universe.

But I've been thinking—that sort of describes almost *every* song. So I guess I'm not really sure about the second book yet.

On the off chance that anything fatal happens to me down here, I need to leave you with a couple of financial instructions. Do you remember the plot of land in Azerbaijan we won at that raffle in Montauk a couple of summers ago? Well, it may be a good time to sell. A consortium of oil companies including British Petroleum, Amoco, and Pennzoil just bought oil fields in the Baku region of the Caspian Sea, and they're planning on running a pipeline into Turkey, which means—if my map is accurate—that they're going to have to come right through our property. I'm sure that Binky knows a realtor over there, but if not, there's probably a Century 21 or a Coldwell Banker in Azerbaijan that can help you.

A few years ago I bought stock in a soft-drink company by the name of Emerald Beverage. The stock hasn't performed particularly well (I bought it at $6 a share and it closed yesterday at $2.25), so you might be tempted to unload it before it drops any further. Try to hold on to it for a bit. The company recently switched ad agencies and they're about to launch a new campaign with a television commercial featuring a coterie of female office workers gathered at a window, mouths agape, leering at a chain gang along the road—the beefy convicts, stripped to the waist in a brutal sun, hack at stones with sledgehammers as sadistic guards guzzle Emerald Diet Cola and occasionally jab the prisoners with rifle butts. The ad's a winner and I think it gives Emerald Beverage stock good upside potential.

Anyway, Merci, I don't want to end with such morbid practicalities. I feel quite safe and I'm doing well. The apartment's slammin'. I'm really enjoying tooling around in the submersible. I get "Frankenstein" cranked up on the system and—sweetie, you'll get a kick out of this— even though it's absolutely desolate down here except for the occasional shrimp or anemone who's strayed from his hydrothermal vent, I put a bumper sticker on the aft ballast tank that says: How's My Driving?

to merci pinto leyner

I miss you and Gaby very much. I adore you both. And I'll be home soon.

Feb. 15, 1995
Challenger Deep,
Mariana Trench

young

bergdorf goodman

brown

The notion to adapt Nathaniel Hawthorne's classic tale "Young Goodman Brown" for the stage and to transpose its physical and temporal settings from a forest on the outskirts of Salem, Massachusetts, in the early 19th century to Bergdorf Goodman, a department store on Fifth Avenue and 57th St. in Manhattan on the eve of the 21st century first occurred to me while I was on a business trip to Los Angeles in March 1994.

I'd gone to L.A. to negotiate the purchase of a chain of hernia clinics. (I already owned eleven hernia clinics across a swath of southeastern Florida running from Miami to Boca Raton up to West Palm Beach which had turned out to be phenomenally lucrative, and I was anxious to expand into other parts of the country.) One day, after a particularly grueling morning session with the seller and our respective attorneys and accountants at my hotel, The

Peninsula in Beverly Hills, needing a respite from the frustrations of trying to analyze the profit margin on an inguinal rupture repair in light of fluctuating reimbursement caps, and facing the prospect of an afternoon of poring over truss swatches, I took a stroll around the block.

There's a beauty salon situated between the Friar's Club and the Beverly Hills YMCA on Santa Monica Blvd. I stood in front of the salon and, through the plate glass window, watched a woman getting a pedicure. The pedicurist was plying an area between the big toe and the second digit of her client's right foot. Working diligently and with considerable exertion, she wielded what looked like some sort of hooked awl or dental pick to dislodge a hard, opalescent plaquelike substance that had occluded the space between the client's toes. (I later learned that the sclerosing deposit was a concretion of bile pigments, cholesterol, and calcium salts, similar in composition to a gallstone.) Given the amount of tissue avulsion and bleeding that this pedicure was producing, one would have assumed that the client was in terrible pain. But there she sat with utter aplomb, serenely perusing a large-print edition of *The Portable Hawthorne*. (I was subsequently able to confirm that the woman's equanimity was the result of an epidural anesthetic.)

And there I stood, the 14-point type clearly legible through the salon's tinted plate glass, reading Hawthorne's "Young Goodman Brown" over the shoulder of, and in prurient tandem with, this recumbent woman who was as oblivious to the peeping Tom with whom she shared the pleasures of her text as she was insensible to the traumas of her Grand Guignol pedicure.

And there, along Santa Monica Blvd., whose sidewalks

were bleached to effulgence by the midday sun and vibrating with 2.0 to 4.5 magnitude aftershocks, the inchoate shards of a play began to coalesce in my mind. I would remake Hawthorne's great parable of evil. But my protagonist would descend not down the footpaths of an encroaching forest, but through the revolving doors of a posh department store. And I would be that bedeviled pilgrim. I would become Young Bergdorf Goodman Brown. And that pilgrim's wife, who, as "Faith" in Hawthorne's original, "thrust her pretty head into the street, letting the wind play with the pink ribbons of her cap" would be my own Merci Pinto, who would "thrust her pretty Ecuadorian head into the street, letting the bus exhaust play with the Blimpie's wrapper she tore from her sub." "Mark," she'd mumble amidst mouthfuls of turkey and provolone, "where the hell are you going at this hour? Bergdorf's is closed. Prithee put off your journey until sunrise, you dumb pendejo."

Young Bergdorf Goodman Brown is not my first play. When I was nine, I wrote and directed a masque which was performed by my Cub Scout pack at my father's Elks Club lodge Christmas party in 1965 in Jersey City, New Jersey. The masque was about a golfer who follows an errant tee-shot into a drainage sluice and discovers a subterranean civilization of technologically advanced gnomes. On the advice of my agent at the time (I've since moved from William Morris to ICM), I expanded it into a full-length three-act. Optioned by a television producer in Burbank, the project was set up with ABC, which planned to package it as one of its Afterschool Specials. Unfortunately, the network insisted that I rewrite the screenplay, expunging any and all references to the golfer's habitual abuse of alcohol and PCP. Manifesting what, with 20/20 hindsight, was the overweening sanctimoniousness and business naïveté of a nine-year-old, I became adamant about the centrality of booze and angel dust to the golfer's character arc, and I proceeded to make several very damaging and completely unsubstantiated charges about craven network executives knuckling under to pressure from the PGA. After pelting a story editor with my own dung in response to her conciliatory suggestion that I simply "tone down" the golfer's chemical abuse, the project was terminated. That afternoon, instead of returning home as my mom tearfully pleaded with me to do, I demanded that the taxi driver take us to the Howard Johnson's in Times Square where, in a pathetic scene recalling Dylan Thomas's 18 whiskies at the White Horse, I scarfed down 26 straight cups of New England clam chowder and collapsed.

This debacle, befalling me at such a vulnerable age, was an aesthetic trauma from which I didn't recover for some time. I developed an extreme aversion to the dramatic form, which persisted until 1972 when—sixteen years old and returning from the Bayreuth Festival with my first wife—I began work on an opera. Tragically, I was only able to complete the following stage setting and character description:

A flooded basement containing the stored furniture, clothing, and miscellaneous jetsam and exotica of an extended family.

Various individuals, waist-deep in the cellar's greasy iridescent water, are wading desultorily, in search of recognizable and salvageable items.

These characters include:

FRANK, owns a deli, heavily in debt to loan sharks, larynx crushed, communicates via deck of flip cards.

TERRI, married to Frank, gorgeous, severely retarded, verbal and cognitive abilities of a two-year-old child.

BABY MAGRINO, Frank's younger sister, a Jew for Jesus, alternates between periods of autistic aphasia and periods of garrulous, nymphomaniacal exuberance (as the action of the opera begins, she is in an impenetrably insular, mute phase).

WILLA, Terri's speech therapist, in love with Frank, a freak abnormality of the cornea and lens has given her microscopic vision, but deprived her of the ability to see any object larger than two micrometers; although she is able to describe the expression on the face of a dust mite or count the number of platelets in a drop of blood, she is considered legally blind by The Department of Motor Vehicles.

After several months of false starts, dead-ends, and agonizingly fruitless labor, I aborted the project, which ended up costing me my marriage and two and a half feet of large intestine.

Given the foregoing history, you probably wonder why I ever contemplated attempting *Young Bergdorf Goodman Brown* in the first place.

I used to go to an amusement park in Wildwood down on the Jersey shore. The most popular attraction for the anomic disaffected teens who habituated the park each summer appeared—at first glance—to be the most innocuous kiddie ride one could imagine: a fire engine, a daffodil, a school bus, a yellow taxi, a little airplane, and a lily pad slowly circling to calliope music. But under one randomly selected vehicle was an ejection system akin to those installed in fighter jets. The location of this ejector was automatically shuffled after each ride. Ejected passengers were shot some 200 feet into the air over the parking lot and came hurtling down either on the hoods of parked cars or more frequently splattering the macadam itself. I knew of only one kid who'd survived an ejection. His name was Donald Bauman. Donald was grievously injured and left a quadriplegic with severe brain damage. But on any given night during the summer, there would be Big Seymour, Donald's best friend, hoisting Donald's limp body onto the daffodil—that was Donald's favorite. Night after night, again and again and again, Donald queued up and took his chance. Finally, one evening, appalled and yet drawn somehow to this behavior, I confronted Donald. "Why?" I asked him. He used a stick in his mouth to peck out four simple words on the special keyboard that was attached to his wheelchair: "Peer pressure and Satan."

I don't know how the odds against writing a play that will be both an artistic and a box-office success compare with the odds against surviving a ride on the daffodil or the lily pad, but I'd echo Peter's succinct justification.

Having successfully completed my negotiations to acquire the hernia clinic franchise in southern California, I returned from L.A. and, to gird myself for work on *Young Bergdorf Goodman Brown,* I decided to pay a visit to my mentor, my former English professor from Brandeis University, Dr. Philip Edelstein.

Edelstein, who is now seventy-three, is being held at the Federal Correctional Institution in Allenwood, Pennsylvania, where he's serving fifteen years for aggravated plagiarism.

When I got to the visitors' room, Edelstein, dressed in prison khakis and sneakers, was already seated and waiting, phone in hand, in one of the partitioned cubicles. I picked up the receiver on my side of the glass.

"How ya doin', Doc?" I asked the erstwhile holder of the Reuben and Irene Davidoff Chair.

"Mezzo mezzo," he replied, with an equivocal flutter of the hand.

I brought him up to speed on the YBGB project and admitted that I was experiencing some trepidation about its feasibility. (Assuming that our conversation was being monitored, I thought it prudent to use initials and words like *feasibility*.)

"Mark, I can't quite recall if you're aware of my family background—"

For the twenty some-odd years that I've known Philip Edelstein, this has been his invariable preamble to almost any response. I knew it word for word.

"Ethnically, we are Samoan Jews, although we have lived—I should say *thrived*—in the greater Antwerp metropolitan area for some eleven generations. I might add that we are not considered 'Jews' by the orthodox Jewish community, nor are we generally regarded as 'Samoan' by expatriate Samoans, and we are certainly not and have never been treated as bona fide 'Belgians.' So I must say, first off, that I have a unique, familial understanding of trepidation."

"Well, thank you, Dr. Edelstein, I find that very comforting."

"Now, my intuitive sense is that you're frightened of finding your protagonist trapped—figuratively or perhaps literally—in this department store without some narrative means of extrication. The question—which extrapolated from its practical application becomes an almost existential quandary—is: How does one get *out* of Bergdorf Goodman? And I have the answer."

"How?" I asked, holding the phone between my cheek and shoulder and quickly flipping my notepad to a fresh page.

"The Mossad."

"The Mossad? The Israeli intelligence agency? That Mossad?"

"That Mossad," he said, nodding gravely.

I should have known. The Mossad was Edelstein's standard deus ex machina. Early in his career he'd received tremendous acclaim for his adaptations of English and American classics which were almost verbatim recapitulations of the original texts except that at the very ends of the books, he would insert the Mossad into the narratives as a means of sudden resolution. In his version of *Moby Dick* for instance, before Ahab has his opportunity, the whale is killed by specially trained Israeli frogmen. In Edelstein's *Wuthering Heights,* a remote-controlled bomb blows up a carriage carrying Heathcliff and Isabella from the Heights to Thrushcross Grange. Although the Israeli government denies any involvement, there is a consensus within the intelligence community that the explosion has the "fingerprints" of a Mossad operation. More recently, Edelstein began to take on works of current fiction which unfortunately resulted in criminal convictions and his imprisonment. Both adaptations of Nicholson Baker's *Vox* and Robert James Waller's *The Bridges of Madison County* were, as usual, almost word-for-word clones of the originals until their closing pages. In Edelstein's *Vox,* before the phone-sex interlocutors can climax, both lines go eerily dead—after we hear two dampened pops, the 9-mm rounds from the silenced automatic pistols of Mossad operatives. And at the very end of Edelstein's *The Bridges of Madison County,* it's revealed that Francesca Johnson, the Iowa farm wife, is in fact a Mossad agent, and her dispatching of photographer Robert Kincaid is so grisly that it compelled a jury to append the crime of heinous revision to the original charge of simple plagiarism.

"Thank you so much, Dr. Edelstein," I said. "I'll certainly keep the Mossad in mind."

He shrugged. "It usually works for me. Listen, my family has a little pied-à-terre in Antwerp that's vacant at the moment. Why don't you fly over and use it to work on the play?"

"That's very generous of you, Doc. But, Merci had her heart set on Mauritius. I thought I'd take the family and work on *Young Bergdorf Goodman Brown* over there."

"Mauritius? Mauritius may be an essay-writing sort of place, perhaps a short story–writing sort of place, but it's no playwriting place. Antwerp is a playwriting place. And anyway, Antwerp is so especially lovely this time of year. It's eel season, and there's the Diamond-Cutting Festival."

I assured him that I'd give his offer serious consideration, thanked him profusely for his help on the play, and we hung up. I watched him shamble over to one of the guards, who escorted him back to his cell.

I couldn't make up my mind about where to go. Merci was really psyched about Mauritius, but I had a feeling that my mentor was right about Antwerp being more conducive to dramatic writing. So I compromised. I decided that we'd all go to Mauritius and that I'd commute to Belgium every other day to work on the play. Including connecting flights, customs, and taxi cabs, travel time between our hotel in Mauritius and Edelstein's apartment in

Antwerp was about 22 hours. This meant, of course, that most of *Young Bergdorf Goodman Brown* was written on airplanes or in airports. Nonetheless, with the exception of a bit of dialogue in the final act, I completed the play on the very day we were scheduled to return to the States.

We flew into Miami so that I could have a quick meeting with the medical director of my hernia clinics down there. We got in early Saturday morning. Somehow that night, I ended up in a suite at the Fontainebleau with Oprah Winfrey, Clarissa Pinkola Estés and Linda Bloodworth-Thomason, playing strip-poker with a deck of Richard Simmons's "Deal-A-Meal" cards. When I got back to our hotel I was just too keyed up to sleep. So I turned on the PowerBook and knocked off that unfinished sequence in the fourth act. And *Young*—or perhaps I should say—*Neonatal Bergdorf Goodman Brown,* conceived in broad daylight on Santa Monica Blvd. in Beverly Hills, California, was born at 4:20 A.M. Sunday, May 1, at the Raleigh Hotel, Miami Beach, Florida.

Young Bergdorf Goodman Brown was first performed at the Almeida Theatre, London, on 10 March 1995.

The cast was as follows:

MARK	Michael de Souza
CLAIRE	Ainslie Hodge
JANICE	Yvonne Meyer
FABIAN	Dietrich Lipper
NEWSCASTER	Jayni Wagner
WOODY	Robert Kern
STEPHANIE	Barbara Fabricant
SHOPPER	Dorothea St. John
JERRY	Kit Stanton
RABBI	George Margoles
TINA	Sharyn Block
SERVER	Brooke Rattray
WAITRESS	Marjorie Moss
PHYLLIS	Ellen Geszel
YOSSI	Andrew Weiss
SIMCHA	Adam Gatewood
Director	Ned Blume
Designer	Peter Schlossberg

act   o n e

MARK
Excuse me, ma'am. Do you work here?

CLAIRE
Yes, I do, sir. Can I help you?

MARK
Yes, I'm looking for a . . . you know, you look awfully familiar. What's your name?

CLAIRE
Claire Winik.

MARK
Winik?

27

CLAIRE

W-I-N-I-K.

MARK

Yeah . . . I knew a Joel Winik in high school. Columbia High School in Maplewood, New Jersey. We played in a band together called Mental Agassi.

CLAIRE

Really? I had a cousin named Joel who went to Columbia High and he was in several bands—The Tumbril Drivers, Plum Slivovitz, Citizen Cane (which was named in honor of that dude they spanked in Singapore), NIMBY, Pheromone Rhetoric, O-Ring, Squid Inc., What Have You Done to My Mother?, NutSack, The Great Pussy Famine, Soon-Yi Can't Come to the Phone Now (which I think they later shortened to just Fōn), Boutros Boutros Boutros Boutros, Quit Twitching, and Looks Like Flan— but I don't think he ever played with a band called Mental Agassi.

MARK

Do you know if he lived in north Maplewood or south Maplewood?

CLAIRE

I'm not really sure.

MARK

When I was in high school, north Maplewood was pre-dominantly Islamic fundamentalist and south Maplewood was Christian and animist.

CLAIRE

I'm pretty sure Joel's family was animist.

MARK

Well, that's probably it then. It must have been another Joel Winik, because everyone in Mental Agassi was from north Maplewood. Weird though, you look so familiar to me. (CLAIRE *shrugs*.) Oh well. I'm looking for a nice pocketbook for my daughter's Haute Barbie.

CLAIRE

Clothes and accessories for Haute Barbie are right over here. Do you have anything in particular in mind?

MARK

Not really. To tell you the truth, this is usually her mother's department. But she's in Arizona with her field hockey team, believe it or not.

CLAIRE

Your wife is a coach?

MARK

No no no. She works for an insurance agency in Englewood Cliffs, New Jersey, and they have a women's field hockey team that plays other insurance agencies, and her team got into the national semifinals which are being held out in Scottsdale, Arizona. So, here I am.

CLAIRE

Does your daughter's doll need a bag for the evening—something very elegant, very soigné—or a sportier look, something casual, something fun?

MARK

I'd say probably a more elegant look. I think Gaby—that's my daughter—said that her Barbie needed the pocketbook for the Academy Awards.

CLAIRE

The Academy Awards?

MARK

Yeah. My daughter and all her friends made videos using their dolls, and they nominated them for "Academy Awards," and the ceremonies are this Friday night.

CLAIRE

And your daughter is up for an "Oscar," so to speak?

MARK

Well, not my daughter. She was kinda pissed off about that actually. She wasn't nominated for Best Director, but her doll got a Best Actress nomination. I don't blame her for being angry—the movie is very very good, especially in comparison to the ones that were nominated. But, y'know, as a father you have to teach your kids to accept the caprices of awards committees.

CLAIRE

That's a tough lesson to learn. What's your daughter's movie about?

MARK

It's very moving. Did you see *Shadowlands*?

CLAIRE

Yes. Very very sad.

MARK

My daughter's movie is much sadder. It makes *Shadow-lands* look like *Porky's.*

CLAIRE

It must be almost unbearably poignant. What's the plot?

MARK

It's a sort of *Jurassic Park/Terms of Endearment* with a Greek myth/Warhol twist. There's this couple—Gaby's Barbie plays the wife—and they have a baby—a little girl, of course—and they go off to live on this island—sort of like Galápagos—where there are all these prehistoric animals running around. And one day they're having a picnic and this huge pterodactyl comes swooping down and snatches the little girl and they never see her again. And it's just heartbreaking. They show the father playing with the infant's musical mobile and he's weeping . . . very powerful stuff. Anyway, a year or so goes by, and the couple has another baby. And one day the father decides to take the family for a picnic. And believe it or not, they're sitting there and again this huge pterodactyl comes swooping down, snatches the new baby in its gaping maw, and they never see her again. And this keeps happening again and again—the couple emerges from its grief, they have another baby, whom they celebrate as a reaffirmation of life itself, a spiritual rebirth, etc. etc., they decide to go on a picnic, and sure enough the baby is snatched by a ravenous pterodactyl. See, this is the Greek mythological aspect—

the endless reiteration is akin to Sisyphus rolling the rock up the mountain or Tantalus reaching for his grapes in futile perpetuity. And the tragic flaw of the father is that he never learns not to take the babies to the picnic area. And I thought that Gaby did something very daring, very Warholian with the length. It's over seven hours of basically the same sequence repeated over and over and over again—birth, picnic, pterodactyl, musical mobile, weeping. But I think it was just a little too avant-garde for the other kids.

CLAIRE
It would make a cool screen saver—pterodactyls snatching kids and flying off.

MARK
Hmmm.

CLAIRE
OK, why don't we take a look at this catalog and see if there's something here that you like. All the finest designers and handbag makers offer models for Haute Barbie—there's Dooney & Bourke, Daniel Swarovski, Bottega Veneta, MCM, Hermés, Louis Vuitton, Chanel. Look at this one here, isn't that gorgeous? It's called "La Mini-Belle," and it's made by Lana of London exclusively for Haute Barbie.

MARK
It's lovely.

CLAIRE
It comes in black or cognac alligator.

MARK

What are these over here?

CLAIRE

That's the "backpack" look. Very chic, very hip. They're utilitarian and ultrasophisticated at the same time. Very soft supple leathers, exotic reptile skins, natural textures like straw and hemp. Extremely hip. I think your daughter and her Barbie would be very happy with one of these.

MARK

That one's beautiful.

CLAIRE

That's one of my absolute favorites! It's a stunning bag. That's a Giorgio Armani, and it's silk and embellished with what's called "ethnic beading."

MARK

What's something like that gonna run me?

CLAIRE

Let me just check the price list back here . . . OK . . . the Armani backpack-bag for Haute Barbie is . . . $3,450.

MARK

Jesus Christ!

CLAIRE

I realize that sounds a bit pricey. But you have to take into consideration that you're paying for the miniaturization. You're getting an Armani bag that's proportioned down to about a 1/70 scale with all the exquisite detailing and craftsmanship that makes an Armani an Armani. Basically, the smaller you go, the more you pay. I don't know if you're aware of some of the robotic medical micro-Barbies they're making now, but their accessories are astronomically expensive. First of all, these Barbies are extraordinarily tiny—about 1/100th the size of your daughter's Haute Barbie—and they're designed to actually enter the human body and perform surgical procedures. There's the original Angioplasty Barbie, for scouring out clogged arteries. There's Transurethral Barbie, who travels up and down the urethra and does prostatic curettage, biopsies, radical prostatectomies. And then there's this new experimental Brain Graft Barbie they're using to implant fetal tissue into the brains of patients suffering from Parkinson's disease. To give you an idea of the costs we're talking about here—Kenneth Cole and Dow Corning make an equipment tote bag for Transurethral Barbie to carry all her miniaturized catheters, cannulas, scalpels, retractors, needles and sutures, etc. And the tote bag *itself* costs $75,000! Just the bag! Now, granted, it's a gorgeous bag—polyurethane, Teflon polyetrafluoroethylene fiber and polyacetal resin. It comes in "transparent" which is very hip, very avant-garde, and I think you can also get it in teal and Nile green. And this is a bag that would look just as elegant at a dinner party or a soirée as it does in the urethra. So when you consider what's out there, the $3,450 doesn't really seem exorbitant at all.

MARK
Yeah, that's true. Do you have the Armani bag in stock?

CLAIRE
If not, I can special-order it for you and have it shipped to

your home within the week. Your daughter's Academy Awards gala is this Friday night, right? So that shouldn't be a problem at all. Let me go check on it now. In the meantime, we have a wonderful Book Department right around the bend over there. Why don't you browse a bit and I'll come find you as soon as I have the bag.

The Book Department.

JANICE
Sir, can I be of any assistance?

MARK
I'm just browsing while I wait for something from another department. Thanks, though.

JANICE
Can I recommend something to you very quickly? I don't know whether or not you're interested in metaphysics, but I think that this new book *Passing Through* is just extraordinary. Are you familiar with it at all?

MARK
No. What's it about?

JANICE
It's 200 individual accounts of people resuscitated from near-death states. It really changes the way you think about death—I mean instead of considering it, y'know, like The End, you start realizing that it's this incredible metamorphosis, and you realize that life is essentially—I

know this is a weird word to use, but I get very entomological when I talk about spirituality—that life is essentially *larval,* and that death is sort of . . .

MARK

Pupal?

JANICE

Yeah, exactly! Pupal. Y'know, this transitional, intervening journey between our immature corporeal phase and our ultimate, eternal being. And the journey can be so beautiful and so mystical. Can I read you something from *Passing Through*? This is the near-death account of a 47-year-old racing driver who suffered multiple head injuries after his Chevrolet spun out of control and slammed into a retaining wall during a practice run for the Daytona 500, and doctors in the emergency room found traces of degermed yellow cornmeal, coconut oil, sugar, salt, whey, romano cheese, cheddar cheese, buttermilk, tomato, monosodium glutamate, onion, baking soda, parmesan cheese, garlic, partially hydrogenated soybean oil, citric acid, red 40, lactic acid, disodium phosphate, paprika, disodium inosinate, and disodium guanate on the fingertips of his driving gloves—which are the ingredients in Bugles Nacho Cheese Corn Snacks—so they determined that he was eating Bugles, dropped the bag, went fishing for it on the floor, and lost control of his car just as he approached the track's high-banked fourth turn and crashed into the wall head on. Do you remember this from the news?

MARK

Yeah, I think so. After the accident, didn't the FDA try to require General Mills to label bags of Bugles with a warning against consuming the chips while operating vehicles traveling over 190 miles per hour?

JANICE

Well they tried, but eventually they were forced to settle for this watered-down "advisory" that said something like "Eating Bugles Nacho Cheese Corn Snacks while negotiating steeply banked turns at speeds in excess of 190 mph has been implicated as a possible health hazard in several epidemiological studies." Like that's really gonna deter anyone. Anyway, this guy's lying in an IC unit in a hospital in Daytona Beach, Florida, he's about to be declared legally deceased, and he has this incredible experience of floating above the bed and then being immersed in what he describes as a "sitz bath of radiant white light," and then he feels himself being thrown into the trunk of a car with diplomatic plates, but the trunk is suffused with this warm effulgence that makes him feel more at peace than he's ever felt before, and soon he's at this whitewashed bougainvillea-draped villa where he's given a polygraph test and even though his responses are predominantly untruthful, he passes the test by using this sphincter-muscle trick he personally learned from William Casey, the former director of the CIA—this is *so* weird, because in life he'd never even met William Casey, never mind get sphincter lessons from the guy—and then he hears this seraphic voice which says: "Go to the House of Kimchi," so he goes to the House of Kimchi, which is this very opulent edifice, sort of like Versailles except that it's completely constructed out of kimchi, those very pungent Korean pickles, and when he arrives there's tremendous commotion going on and he sees this woman sprawled out on the lawn in her bra and jeans and she's choking

"There's no air in there—just air freshener!" and the racing driver is like "Who sprayed the place, the authorities?" and she's gasping, "Yeah, they put tank turrets through the walls and they pumped the air freshener in," so he rushes into the House of Kimchi and begins to inhale the air freshener, which is like this beautiful aerosol iridescence, and he describes it as "inhaling the sparkling light until there was no distinction between the radiance of the air freshener and myself—we were one." Isn't that incredible? And the even more amazing thing is how close this is—and I mean detail to detail—to most of the other accounts.

MARK
Do you really believe that stuff? Near-death accounts always sound to me like those *Penthouse Forum* letters.

JANICE
I was suspicious myself, but then I found out that every single account in *Passing Through* had been certified by a notary public. I don't blame you for being skeptical, though. There's a lot of totally bogus information out there. I guess that's one of the things I like about insects and worms so much—their honesty. But hey, that's my own issue. I doubt that most other people have ever thought about a tsetse fly or a leech in terms of its candor.

MARK
I think it's just a matter of not having the time. Y'know, we're all so damn busy every minute. Say I happen upon a termite, for instance. I'm usually up against some sort of writing deadline or running off to some appointment or another, and he seems just as hectic—foraging for wood,

grooming his antenna, dragging the corpse of some fallen compadre back to the nest, whatever. So there just isn't the opportunity for us to sit down quietly and have any kind of meaningful interaction. Y'know what I mean?

JANICE

Well, I just find it ridiculous how society makes these arbitrary, completely subjective classifications for forms of life. Like, OK, you're *noble;* you over there, you're *adorable;* and you under there, you're *vile and repugnant.* There's a wonderful passage about all this in a new book we just got in . . . Where is it? . . . OK, here we go. Listen to this:

> It's a gorgeous summer morning in central Florida. Donald and Kelly Weber and their two children Alex and Chelsea are in their cobalt-green 1995 Toyota Camry, midway between Lake Helen and Cassadaga, heading west on Interstate 4 toward Orlando and their ultimate destination: The Walt Disney World Resort Complex.
>
> Suddenly, a male and female Aeshinid dragonfly *(Anax junius)*—clasped in copulatory flight and en route to a stagnant pond where the female intends to deposit her fertilized eggs—swoops in front of the oncoming Camry. The impact between windshield and dragonflies is catastrophic, obliterating the spawning mother and her amorous mate. Where once there was life, perhaps even love, now is a gob of viscera, spreading slightly across the tinted glass and then congealing in the head wind.
>
> The Webers—loving parents, tax-paying, law-abiding, recycling suburbanites—are oblivious. Giddy with the looming proximity of Disney World, they are

unaware that a fatal collision has taken place. Later, at an Exxon station, Don will unceremoniously squee-gee away the remains of this most undistinguished road-kill.

If you found it easy to assume the role of the blithe Webers in the foregoing scenario, you're not alone. In a recent poll conducted by the Automobile Association of America (AAA), some 97 percent of those surveyed said that they felt "little or no remorse" about the in-sects they've slain with their cars.

What is it in our sociopsychological makeup that makes the death of an insect so inconsequential? Why have different cultures diverged so dramatically in con-ferring status on their zoological brethren? How odd, for instance, and perfectly inverse to our own valua-tion, that the ancient Nazca of southern Peru revered the anchovy as an aquatic shaman and yet considered the dolphin suitable as a topping for their *hulponob,* a flat corn cake spread with goat curds, a kind of proto-pizza.

MARK

That's fascinating. I had no idea the Nazca invented pizza. What's that from?

JANICE

It's from the introduction of this terrific new book by an Australian entomologist by the name of Dr. Astrid Swain called *Do Lice Laugh? The Inner World of the Phthirius Pubis.* Swain put a classified ad in a Brisbane newspaper offering men with crabs—y'know, pubic lice—a modest stipend for participating in a research project. And she found a suitable subject, this itinerant laborer who's called "Eric" in the book—I don't think that's his real name—and Eric set up residence in her laboratory and, for a year, Dr. Swain studied his lice right in their natural habitat. I think that one of the things that distinguishes this book—and you might disagree with me about this—is that Dr. Swain is a woman, and I think that enabled her to empathize and connect emotionally with the lice in ways that I believe would have been impossible for a man. This is no abstract disquisition. This is a very poignant, very personal chronicle of the lives of thousands upon thousands of pubic lice—you have to realize that lice reproduce very rapidly, nits hatch every seven to ten days. And to give you an indication of Swain's approach, she names each and every louse: there's Corky and Bopper and Misha and Sleepy and Darnel and Annie and so on. This is a book about what the world looks and feels like to a crab louse. Swain discovers—surprise, surprise—that crab lice fall in love, that crab lice dream, that crab lice get depressed, that crab lice have evolved very sophisticated methods of conflict resolution, etc. etc. And it's also a book about the relationship that develops between Dr. Swain and Eric—the fact that the lice colonize Eric's pubic hair necessitates a fairly intimate day-to-day interaction. And I think one of the things that people will find particularly admirable is the very tactful, very delicate manner in which Dr. Swain discusses Eric's anatomy. There's never the slightest hint of salaciousness or lapse into cheap humor. And another thing I really loved about the book is how up-front Swain was about the project's conclusion, which was very acrimonious. Apparently before Swain was ready to terminate the research, Eric decided that he just couldn't stand the lice anymore and he had a friend sneak a bottle of Kwell into the lab and he exterminated the colony. Swain was devastated—she'd become profoundly attached to the lice, of course, but she was also terribly hurt that Eric would make a decision of that magnitude unilaterally. So they didn't part on particularly good terms. But Dr. Swain's analysis of their estrangement is illuminating in and of itself. I have one minor quibble with the book, well, with the photographs—I think the black bar they always put over Eric's eyes gives the photos this stag-film look that's completely inappropriate. But otherwise, I recommend *Do Lice Laugh?* wholeheartedly. Oh, and I almost forgot— it's also available as an interactive hypertext CD-ROM, and we have versions for both Windows and MAC.

MARK
This Astrid Swain is some formidable researcher, huh?

JANICE
She reminds me a lot of an anthropology professor I had at Brandeis. Absolutely fearless. Here was this tiny erudite woman who'd come to class in her pince-nez and prim shirtwaist dresses, and then show us videos of herself snorting ebene with the Yanomamö, sniffing glue with street gangs in Rio, swilling home-brewed vodka with salvage crews at Chernobyl . . . And we'd be like, whoa!

MARK
You went to Brandeis?

JANICE
Class of 1989.

MARK

That's such a coincidence. I went to Brandeis, too. But I graduated back in '77.

JANICE

Slightly before my time. But you might have known my brother—he also went to Brandeis and graduated in the late seventies.

MARK

No kidding? What's his name?

JANICE

Mitchell Syrkin.

MARK

You gotta be kidding! Mitchell Syrkin? I knew Mitchell Syrkin very well. In my sophomore year, Mitch lived in the same dorm, right down the hall from me. In fact, I'll never forget the first time I met Mitch Syrkin. It was the beginning of the semester, a bunch of us were hanging out in my dorm room, there's a knock on the door and here's this flaxen-haired Adonis, big smile, beautiful white teeth, gorgeous clothes—and we just all look at each other like, who's this jerk? We absolutely despised him! And of course soon we find out that he's probably the hardest-working, most considerate and generous guy any of us had ever met in our lives!

JANICE

Hard-working? Generous? I don't think it's even remotely possible to describe my brother as either hard-working or generous. Docile, anxious, ineffectual, high-strung, self-absorbed, not capable of interest in other people, emotionally dependent, amoral, demanding of attention, given to lying and short-lived enthusiasms, slovenly, impulsive, impressionable, mercurial, hypochondriac, perverted, easily bored, craves novelty, and becomes frustrated by the slightest obstacle—maybe. But hard-working and generous—no way.

MARK

You sure?

JANICE

Absolutely. And another thing—Mitchell was never a "flaxen-haired Adonis." He's always had slimy black hair. And the word I'd use to best describe my brother's physique is *suety*.

MARK

Suety? Oh, well. I guess it was another Mitch Syrkin. Weird though, huh? Brandeis, late seventies . . .

Enter CLAIRE.

CLAIRE

Mr. Leyner, sorry I was so long. Good news, though. We have the Armani backpack-bag for Haute Barbie in stock. For some reason it was sent down to Men's Apparel—don't ask me why. So if you go down to Sub 6 and go to Men's Apparel and ask for Fabian, he should have the bag and you'll be all set.

MARK

Sub 6?

CLAIRE

That's Subterranean 6. We're on the ground level. You just need to take that elevator over there six floors down. OK?

MARK

OK. Thanks a lot.

a   c   t   t w o

Sub 6. Men's Apparel.

MARK

Are you—

FABIAN

Fabian Spivak, sir. And you must be Mr. Leyner.

MARK

Yes, I am. There's an Armani backpack-bag for my daughter's Haute Barbie that was sent down here . . .

FABIAN

It's apparently en route, Mr. Leyner.

MARK

Do you know how long it's going to take?

FABIAN

It should be here momentarily. Can I get you a cup of coffee while you wait?

MARK

You know what I could really go for? A daiquiri. And a pack of True Menthols.

FABIAN

(Tears of laughter streaking his mascara.) I'll see what I can do.

MARK

Fabian, did you say your last name is Spivak?

FABIAN

Yes, sir.

MARK

About fifteen, sixteen years ago, right after I got out of graduate school, I worked as an advertising copywriter for a company called AVP—Ando Veterinary Pharmaceuticals—in Secaucus, New Jersey. And there was another copywriter there by the name of . . . I think something like Marla . . . no, Marcia . . . Marcia Spivak.

FABIAN

I have a sister Salome whose nickname is Marcia who once worked in advertising. I'm not sure exactly where, though. It was years ago.

MARK

I wonder if it could be the same one? Was her first husband, by any chance, a feminine-hygiene products industry analyst for PaineWebber?

FABIAN

Marcia's first husband originally worked for Tambrands, which is a feminine-hygiene products company—they make Tampax—and then I think he *did* become an industry analyst, but I'm fairly certain that it was for Morgan Stanley, not PaineWebber.

MARK

Hmmmm . . . it could have been Morgan Stanley, I suppose. Did your sister then marry a much older man, I think a teak importer, who mysteriously disappeared and whose body was found months later in a cranberry bog down near . . . I think it was Rehoboth Beach, Delaware?

FABIAN

No, sir. Marcia divorced her first husband, whose name was Mort Perlbinder—

MARK

That's right.

FABIAN

—and then she became very involved in the right-to-life movement—not the antiabortion wing, but the antieuthanasia wing—and, through her work in the movement, she fell in love with a brain-dead teenager by the name of Jeffrey Schlein who was being kept breathing by a ventilator in a hospital down in Roanoke, Virginia, and she tried to marry him.

MARK
That's right, that's right. And there was a tremendous amount of controversy about the marriage, wasn't there?

FABIAN
Well, first of all, my parents were totally opposed to it because of the age difference—my sister was in her early thirties at the time and this kid Jeff was only sixteen. And second of all, in Virginia, when there is irreversible cessation of the functioning of the centers in the brainstem that control the breathing, pupillary, and other vital reflexes, the person is declared legally dead. And, in Virginia, it's a crime to marry a dead person.

MARK
Isn't it illegal to marry a brain-dead minor in every state?

FABIAN
I think it's legal in Nevada. But anyway, all of this became completely moot when she met this other guy Alan Wasserman and fell in love with him.

MARK
He was a Malaysian kickboxer, right?

FABIAN
He's an anesthesiologist. I think originally from Utica.

MARK
You sure?

FABIAN

I'm quite sure.

MARK

You're absolutely certain that Marcia's present husband is an anesthesiologist from Utica and not a Malaysian kickboxer?

FABIAN

There's no question about it. Marcia met Alan Wasserman at the hospital in Roanoke—in fact, Alan Wasserman un-plugged Jeffrey.

MARK

It wasn't your sister, then. The Marcia Spivak I worked with in the advertising department at AVP is married to a Malaysian kickboxer. I'm positive because I was just re-cently with a group of friends and we were watching Southeast Asian Corporal Punishment on pay-per-view—I don't know if you know this, but convicted rapists in Malaysia are kicked in the testicles fifteen times by a mar-tial artist, before their genitals are immersed in a tank of piranha—and here's this kickboxing champion limbering up, breaking cinder blocks and whatnot, and then they show his wife in the audience, this patrician-looking woman wearing a gorgeous black dress by Jil Sander—

FABIAN

The one with the sheer chiffon panels?

MARK

No, it had big ribbons that trailed in the back sort of like birds' plumes. Anyway, I went completely nuts! I was jumping up and down, screaming, "That's Marcia from AVP! That's Marcia from AVP!"

FABIAN
And you're definitely sure it was the same woman?

MARK
Definitely. We worked very closely together on a major launch campaign. In certain African countries, they have a terrible problem with vulture droppings knocking out high-tension wires. So Ando Veterinary Pharmaceuticals developed a vulture stool softener as a means of protecting power lines in these regions. Now this was a remarkable feat of R&D because, as it turns out, it's nearly impossible to medicate the vultures directly, so the medicinal agent has to be ingested by the animals who will eventually become the carrion upon which the vultures feed.

FABIAN
So we're talking about a delivery system that entails a fairly complex ecosystemic intervention.

MARK
Exactly. Anyway, EATO—the East African Telecommunication Organization—convened a meeting in Mombasa, Kenya, to address this whole problem with the high-tension wires, which gave AVP a perfect opportunity to pitch its new product directly to the appropriate energy and wildlife ministry officials. So the advertising department was given the assignment to produce a ten-minute marketing video, which Marcia and I were responsible for writing. And I must say, Fabian, I think we did a damn good job. The video opens up with a beautiful shot of vul-

tures wheeling over a wildebeest carcass on the savannah, and then we cut to a tight shot of the vultures consuming medicated carrion, and then we show them taking flight one-by-one in slow-motion and soaring gracefully on thermal updrafts over the high-tension wires, and then we dissolve to footage of a chortling Masai family watching "Three's Company," uninterrupted by power outages. And the soundtrack was marvelous. Marcia and I came up with the idea to get Depeche Mode to do this vibrant splashy version of Respighi's "La boutique fantasque." And it just really worked. Apparently they went nuts in Mombasa.

FABIAN
Mr. Leyner, I don't know what in God's name is taking so long with your daughter's Barbie accessory. Why don't I try to find out what's going on, and in the meantime, perhaps you'd like to try on a few things. We just got in the *Swords into Plowshares* line for men that everyone's been raving about.

MARK
What is that?

FABIAN
Well, it all started with a sort of facetious gauntlet flung down from the White House. About a year ago, Vice President Gore, addressing The National Competitiveness Council of the Defense Industry Alliance, admonished the assembled honchos that the post–Cold War geostrategic configuration necessitated rapid transition to peacetime applications—a "swords to plowshares" diversification—if the country's top defense contractors were going to re-

main competitive in the global marketplace. And, in what was really a tongue-in-cheek challenge, Gore asked: "If the exigencies of the marketplace suddenly required you to produce men's and women's ready-to-wear apparel instead of high-tech weaponry, who among you would be agile enough to respond?" Well, this was a pretty proud and feisty bunch of businessmen who didn't appreciate the insinuation—however jocular—that they were a bunch of lumbering dinosaurs. So they decided to call the Vice President's bluff. And voilà—designed, manufactured, and on store shelves in less than a year—you've got your full line of *Swords into Plowshares* apparel.

MARK

Is there anything you recommend especially?

FABIAN

Let's take a look here . . . Oh this is a gorgeous suit right here. This is from Lockheed—it's a pale blue double-breasted, pin dot two-piece tropical wool suit. Very gorgeous. And somewhere here I've got a slate cotton gauze dress shirt from Grumman that would work beautifully . . . Oh, Mr. Leyner, you have to try this on—this is a single-breasted, three button linen-and-viscose glen-plaid suit from McDonnell Douglas—y'know, they make the F/A-18 naval attack jet. This is an absolutely exquisite suit.

MARK

It's a beautiful suit.

FABIAN

Are you familiar with Northrop? They make the TSSAM (AGM-137) Cruise Missile. This is their madras unconstructed sportcoat. That's a very fresh look, isn't it? They also do a mandarin-collar linen jacket that's very, very stylish. Let's see . . . I don't know if you need underwear or not, but Martin Marietta puts out a line of boxer shorts that's terrific fun. Let's see, let's see . . . here we go—this would make a very cheeky casual outfit. This is a heather-gray cotton V-neck cardigan from Raytheon which I think works really well with these Rockwell International oversize denim painter pants—you don't even need a shirt under the sweater. I think you get a very breezy, very nonchalant look, streetwise but without the grunge. We've got ties—Thiokol makes some beautiful patterned silk ties . . . Why don't I pull some things for you to try on while I go see what's taking so long with your daughter's Barbie bag? What are you, Mr. Leyner, about a 15/34 shirt and a 38 suit?

MARK

In shirts I take a 15 neck with a 33-inch sleeve, and I'm a 37 short suit with a 32-inch waist.

FABIAN

OK. Here we go. Why don't you just follow me over here . . . Y'know we have speakers in the dressing rooms. Is there anything you'd like to hear—classical, jazz, country, new age, alternative, house, techno, metal, rap, reggae, ska, zydeco, news radio, books-on-tape?

MARK

How about the news?

FABIAN

You got it.

★ ★ ★

Dressing room. MARK *is trying on clothes.*

RADIO NEWS BROADCAST

Arts groups and the ACLU have blasted Senator Jesse Helms for his attempts to deny NEA funding to a Miami publishing collective that has produced a controversial and, in the words of the North Carolina senator, "morally repugnant" calendar.

The calendar, entitled "Transgressive Tableaux," depicts explicit and often sadomasochistic acts between live models and illustrated iconic figures. The month of December features a head-shaven, heavily muscled black man cracking an amyl nitrate capsule under his nose as he's sodomized by a grinning Santa Claus. July boasts a naked woman wearing what appear to be mousetraps on her nipples, squatting over Uncle Sam, his beard suffused with the yellow of her urine.

"This writhing moral indignation is a complete masquerade," said Brett Wheeler from the Arts Freedom Coalition. "I seriously doubt that Helms ever complained to his plumbing contractor that the nude woman with her legs wrapped around a polyvinyl chloride vent pipe on *his* calendar was 'repugnant.'"

Irvin Dorsey, a spokesman for the National Plumbing Association, an industry lobbying group, called Wheeler's remarks "insensitive."

"The implication that all plumbers are sexist troglodytes who spend their working hours leering at titillating pinups is an affront to tens of thousands of hard-working men *and*

women in the plumbing, heating, ventilating, and air-conditioning industry."

In a related incident, Kraft General Foods Inc. has apologized to hundreds of food retailers who mistakenly received the "Transgressive Tableaux" calendar in the mail instead of the "Kraft Kitchen Holiday Calendar."

Cheryl Knapp, Vice President for Public Affairs at Kraft General Foods, issued the following statement: "Someone in the mail room obviously thought it was a joke to mix this pornography in with our complementary holiday mailing. We at Kraft assure our customers that we do not find it amusing. We deeply regret any discomfort or embarrassment this incident may have caused, and we promise to identify, dismiss, and, if possible, prosecute the individual or individuals responsible to the fullest extent of the law."

Edwin Sanchez, president of the National Office Workers Union, expressed his organization's anger over Knapp's statement: "The fact that, without any corroborating evidence, Kraft immediately assumes that it was a mail room worker who committed this act clearly shows an unacceptable bias against our membership."

MARK

Fabian . . . Fabian!!

FABIAN

Yes, Mr. Leyner.

MARK

Fabian, I changed my mind. Could you put something else on? What books-on-tape do you have?

FABIAN

Let me check . . . OK, the only books-on-tape we seem to have right now are *Baby Names for the '90s* by Barbara Kay Turner, as read by Liam Neeson, and *Magic Eye,* which is that book of color designs that reveal surprising images when you stare at them in certain ways.

MARK

Do you have any of those aural environment CDs—something nice and soothing?

FABIAN

We have something called *Tranquility I*—it's the sound of Cindy Crawford's legs being waxed, but slowed way down, so you get this very peaceful *whoosh.* I believe that was recorded in Dharmsala, India. And we have *Tranquility II,* which is the sound of gnocchi being dropped into boiling water. And I think that one's actually sped up slightly, so you get a continuous softly plopping kind of Zen effect.

MARK

Either one's fine.

FABIAN

You got it. And I've put a trace-call into Inventory, so we should be hearing any minute about the bag.

FABIAN *exits.*

Enter WOODY HOCHSWENDER, *Editor of* Esquire Gentleman.

WOODY
Mark, are you in there?

MARK
Who's that?

WOODY
It's Woody Hochswender.

MARK
Woody, what are you doing here?

WOODY
I'm looking for you. Where the hell have you been for the past couple of days?

MARK
What do you mean?

WOODY
Three days ago, I called you at home. Merci answered and told me that she was on her way to Arizona for a field hockey tournament and that you were on your way out the door to go to Bergdorf Goodman to buy Gaby a pocketbook for her Barbie.

MARK
Three days ago? You mean I've been here for three days? Weird.

WOODY

What are you doing in there?

MARK

Trying on clothes. Have you ever seen these Martin Marietta boxer shorts. Really nice. They're 50% cotton, 50% Stealthon—which is this new synthetic fabric that enables you to penetrate radar undetected.

WOODY

Listen, the reason I've been trying to get in touch is that we're about to close the new issue of *Esquire Gentleman* and I want to go over the revisions I made in your column with you.

MARK

I still have a couple of things to try on, Woody. Why don't you just read me the changes.

WOODY

All right. I thought we'd title it "Is My One-Year-Old a Criminal?" and then subhead it something like: "Renowned Child Psychologist Mark Leyner Explores the Arcane and Frightening World of Toddler Gangs."

MARK

That sounds fine.

WOODY

I left the body of the text pretty much alone. And in the Q&A section I just switched the order a bit. I thought we'd open with "My little boy can't seem to make up his mind what he wants. One minute he's chasing me around the house, hanging on my legs while I'm trying to get work done. The next, he's trying to get away from me when I sit down to hug him. Is this a 'gang thing'?" and close with "My daughter is beginning to develop an imaginary friend. Experts say this is a welcome sign of cognitive development. But what if he's in an imaginary gang?"

MARK

That's cool.

WOODY

Then there's the section about getting older kids, former toddler gang members who've gone straight, to come talk to toddlers at play groups and day care. And you've got an extended quote from that six-year-old named Gideon. Well, I cut that a bit and thought maybe we could use it as a sidebar.

MARK

Good idea.

WOODY

OK. I just want you to hear the revised version:

"When I was eight months old, nine months old, a year . . . I just didn't give a shit. I didn't care about anything. If I didn't like what I was being fed, I just spewed it—carrots, beets, peas—and I didn't care who I hit. Y'know what I'm sayin'? I'd shit in my diaper—it didn't really bother me to crawl around like that. I was like, hey, whatever. Crying, whining—yeah, for hours if I felt like. To me, at that time, just to sit there quietly playing with a shape-sorter toy or watching public television attentively—that just seemed nerdy . . . weak. I was more into screwing up the settings on your TV and VCR or ripping your earring out of your earlobe or swallowing some dimes. If there were magazines on your coffee table and I could get to them—I'd rip those damn magazines apart, page by page. And I didn't care what it was—*Time, Entertainment Weekly, The New Yorker, Scientific American, Martha Stewart Living* . . . I just didn't care. I really didn't see a future beyond that behavior at that time in my life."

MARK

That seems just fine, Woody.

WOODY

Good. I think that ending is so chilling, when he says: "I really didn't see a future beyond that behavior at that time in my life."

MARK

There's a photograph of Gideon, I think he's about eleven months old, and he's sitting in his mom's car, a heavy-lidded expression on his face, and he's "throwing his sign" to another toddler in a car seat—he's got his thumb in his mouth and he's languidly stroking the bridge of his nose with his index finger—signaling his gang affiliation. And talk about chilling—this photograph makes your blood run cold. See if you can get a print from Gideon's mom and maybe you could run it with the sidebar.

WOODY

Good idea. Listen, I gotta run. I'll send you galleys.

Exit WOODY.

Enter FABIAN.

FABIAN

Mr. Leyner. Good news and bad news.

MARK *emerges from the dressing room.*

MARK

What's the story, Fabian?

FABIAN

OK, good news: I've located the Armani backpack-bag for your daughter's Barbie—it got routed somehow to Home Furnishings down on Sub 15. Bad news: all I could find was schnapps and the machine didn't have True Menthols so I got you a pack of Salem Lights.

MARK

That's perfectly fine, Fabian. Thanks. Now, how do I get to Sub 15?

FABIAN

If you walk through this department and then continue straight ahead until you get to an aquamarine glass-brick partition and then make a left, you'll find an elevator that'll take you right down to Sub 15. Go to Home Furnishings and ask for Jerry and he should have the bag.

MARK

Is there a men's fragrance department? As long as I'm here I might as well get some new aftershave.

FABIAN

It's right on the way to the elevator, Mr. Leyner. You can't miss it.

Men's Fragrance Department. Much later.

STEPHANIE

Mr. Leyner, we've run out of places on your body to daub samples. I must say you are one of the most discriminating fragrance customers I've ever met.

MARK

Yeah, I know. I'm very olfactory. But listen, you said there was one more you'd thought I'd really like. There's gotta be a spot somewhere on me that we haven't used?

STEPHANIE

We've daubed your wrists, your lower arms, your upper arms, your chest, your stomach, your ankles, calves, knees . . . Let's see . . . Hey, if you don't mind, how about the upper portion of your buttocks?

MARK

No, I don't mind. You think I'll really like this one, right?

STEPHANIE

It's a very compelling, very expansive, masculine fragrance. Now bend over and pull your shorts down a bit . . . OK, there we go. (STEPHANIE *fans* MARK's *but-*

tocks with a Paco Rabanne point-of-purchase display.) I just want some of the alcohol to evaporate before we smell.

MARK
Steph, how I can smell it back there?

STEPHANIE
Hmmmm . . . How about if we ask that woman over there for her opinion. I think we're both sort of smelled-out anyway.

MARK
OK.

STEPHANIE
Ma'am, excuse me. Would you mind helping us out over here for a second? *(The* SHOPPER *approaches and smiles down at* MARK *who, doubled over, his bare, pale behind cantilevered in the air, smiles back.)* Ma'am, could you smell this right here . . . just that one cheek, ma'am . . . there you go. Now tell me that isn't just lovely.

SHOPPER
Ummmm. That *is* nice. What is it?

STEPHANIE
It's something new from Gianfranco Petronio called "Duce."

STEPHANIE *hands her the box, which depicts exultant neo-fascists cruising Rome's Piazza del Popolo shouting "Duce!" and offering straight-armed salutes.*

SHOPPER

Do you mind if I have another? *(She sniffs.)* Ummm. Ummmmm. It's a kind of black fruit . . . *(she sniffs again)* . . . leather . . . *(she inhales deeply)* . . . roasted nut bouquet. *(She kneels down to address MARK whose flushed inverted face is between his knees.)* Personally, sir, I love it.

MARK

Thanks for your help. Say, do either of you know what floor Home Furnishings is on? Fabian told me, but I think all these colognes have made me a bit lightheaded.

STEPHANIE

Home Furnishings is on Sub 15.

SHOPPER

(Shivers.) Sub 15? Oooh, I never go beneath Sub 10. You get much further down, that's where I've heard that the Jews and the extraterrestrials turn gentiles into those little action figures. It's too scary down there for me . . . personally.

MARK

What? Jews and extraterrestrials turn gentiles into action figures? What are you talking about?

STEPHANIE

(Trying to steer her away.) Thank you so much for all your help, ma'am.

SHOPPER

(Turning back to MARK.) This is what I've heard—the

Jews and the extraterrestrials kidnap gentiles who've defaulted on their charge accounts and then they bring 'em
way down underground under the building here and they
turn them into those little action figures the kids love so
much—y'know, like those Mighty Morphin Power
Rangers or whatever the hell they're called. This is what
I hear.

MARK

That's ridiculous! How do you—

STEPHANIE

(Firmly guiding her away.) Ma'am, again, thank you very
much for your assistance. You have a nice day now.
Bye-bye.

SHOPPER *exits.*

MARK

Do you have any idea what the hell she was talking about?

STEPHANIE

Mr. Leyner, I'm very sorry about that. The woman had a
good nose for cologne but she's obviously a very paranoid
and very gullible individual. Or maybe we're just all getting a little lightheaded from the cologne. *(She laughs.)*
Now, do you remember how to get to the elevator?

MARK

Yeah—aquamarine glass-brick, make a left.

STEPHANIE

That's it. Oh, and Mr. Leyner . . .

MARK

Yes, Stephanie?

STEPHANIE

You can straighten up now.

MARK *stands, pulls up his shorts and trousers, and exits.*

a c t   t h r e e

Sub 15. Home Furnishings.

MARK

Jerry?

JERRY

Good evening, Mr. Leyner. Sorry about the runaround
with your daughter's Barbie pocketbook.

MARK

But you've got it, right?

JERRY

I will very shortly.

MARK

What? I thought it was being sent down here.

JERRY

Well, it was. But then when Fabian up in Men's Apparel called Inventory and they realized that they'd routed it mistakenly down here to Home Furnishings they managed to catch it and they had it sent to Men's Apparel, but by the time it got there you were gone.

MARK

But I was in Men's Fragrance . . . Fabian knew where I'd gone. Why didn't he come get me or have it sent there?

JERRY

Fabian's shift ended at about the time you left Apparel for Fragrance, and Patrick—who comes on after Fabian—I guess didn't know where you'd gone. To be perfectly honest with you, Mr. Leyner, I don't think Patrick even knew who the hell you were or really gave a flying you-know-what about any of this, so . . . Anyway, it's on its way back down here.

MARK

OK.

JERRY

If there's anything here you're curious about, please don't hesitate to ask. We've got some super gift items in. I don't know about you, but I don't think a week goes by where I don't have a wedding or housewarming gift or a birthday present to get someone, so I've always got my eye out for, y'know, neat gift items. It doesn't hurt to stock up, either. That's a little trick I learned from the survivalist magazines. They believe that when Armageddon comes— y'know, the cataclysmic race wars and whatnot—and the streets are running with blood, it's not gonna be so easy to just run out and get a wedding gift for someone. So they advocate stockpiling—accumulating a horde of gift items. I don't necessarily believe all that Book of Revelations stuff, but it's not a bad idea to have a few spare gift items around the house. Am I right?

MARK

That makes sense. Say, Jerry—you don't know anything about Jews and extraterrestrials kidnapping gentiles who've defaulted on their charge accounts and turning them into Mighty Morphin Power Rangers down on one of the lower floors, do you?

JERRY

No, sorry, Mr. Leyner. I just started here a week ago.

MARK

Oh.

JERRY

This is a great item right here. Very exotic. It's a diagnostic tool used in traditional Chinese medicine. Y'know how when you're waiting for the doctor in the exam room and you're sitting on that wax paper on the examination table and your perspiration leaves marks on the paper? Well, instead of using blood work-ups and EKGs and X rays and all that, traditional Chinese doctors analyze these shapes that are left on the paper and they use that to diagnose you. Whereas you might get up from an exam table and see that your thighs left sweat imprints that just look to you like maybe two langostinos, a Chinese physician can look at that and deduce a heart murmur, hypoglycemia, gout, y'know? So you get a 200-ft. roll of the paper and a diagnostic instruction booklet. It's great fun at parties. And we have customers who use it for slip covers, wall hangings, window swagging. It also makes pretty good freezer wrap. Let's see . . . Oh, this is really neat. And very practical. Y'know how when there's any kind of power outage or you blow a fuse and all the digital clocks in your house are blinking 00:00? Well, this is a new electronic reset device that automatically adjusts your microwave and VCR clocks to the Coordinated Universal Time Signal at the National Institute of Standards and Technology at Boulder, Colorado. You like accuracy? We're talkin' full money-back guarantee here. A second takes what—like 9,192,631,000 vibrations of the cesium atom?

MARK

9,192,631,770.

JERRY

Well, if your VCR clock is reset and it's off by even a single cesium atom vibration—you get a complete refund. OK . . . Here's something that's great for parents. Do you have any kids, Mr. Leyner?

MARK

I have a daughter.

JERRY

Well then, you must know how parents love to have keepsakes from their kid's early childhoods, y'know, like their first shoes, their teething rings, their favorite little teddy bears, stuff like that. Well, this is a beautiful lacquer box with a patented liquid-nitrogen refrigeration system that enables you to save your child's umbilical stump, foreskin, baby teeth, tonsils, adenoids, appendix, whatever. Whether it's simply fallen off or it's been surgically removed—if it's from your little one's body, it's too precious to just throw away. As I mentioned, it's got a handsome lacquer shell over high-impact, vandal-resistant plastic and it comes with one optional feature: a radio signal that alerts the owner whenever the door is opened. The signal device can beam information about "unauthorized access" to wristwatch paging devices, personal computers, and a new type of dashboard receiver that can display data. So, say you and your family are driving to the country and someone's broken into your home and is trying to jimmy the box open and make off with your daughter's adenoids—a visual alarm is immediately displayed on your dashboard. I just got one of these for my uncle—he's a butcher over in Jersey, in Hoboken. This guy's a nut for saving everything of his son's: moles, cuticles, his—

MARK
Your uncle's a butcher in Hoboken? I live in Hoboken. Where's your uncle's shop?

JERRY
Washington Street between 9th and 10th.

MARK
You're serious? That's my butcher. I live on 10th and Washington—you're uncle's my butcher!

JERRY

Really?

MARK

It's gotta be the same guy. He was just sick, right? He had an epileptic seizure from playing video games and then he developed Sydenham's chorea, a severe movement disorder in which the arms and legs flail about rapidly and uncontrollably. And he took a few weeks off and went down to Florida and it cleared up pretty much. Right?

JERRY

No. My uncle had a seizure, but he was down at the shore and he was driving down this road that was lined with tall, thin trees that caused the sunlight to have a strobelike effect and *that* gave him an epileptic seizure. And he seemed OK for a little while, but then he developed Noonan's syndrome—a disorder that gave him club feet, a concave chest, droopy eyelids, wooly hair, limited use of his elbows and hydrocephalus—a buildup of fluid that caused an enlarged head. So he went to Palm Springs for about a month, and it all cleared up and he's fine now, knock on wood.

MARK

You're sure it wasn't video games?

JERRY

Strobe effect of sunlight through trees.

MARK

And it wasn't Sydenham's chorea?

JERRY

Noonan's syndrome.

MARK

But it's Washington Street between 9th and 10th?

JERRY

Yup.

MARK

Weird. Really weird.

JERRY

Mr. Leyner, do you wear jewelry?

MARK

Sometimes. Why?

JERRY

You might be interested in this either for yourself or as a gift idea. Y'know those medical alert bracelets people wear so that, in case they're in an accident, paramedics and doctors will know that they're allergic to certain drugs? Well, this is an erotic-alert bracelet. In case, for whatever reason—accident, disease, senility, drugs, alcohol—you become amnesiac or aphasic, this bracelet informs your sexual partners exactly what you like—y'know, what turns you on. It's got an LCD display right here and about 200 kilobytes of memory, so you can include fairly elaborate instructions or scenarios. You might need your partner to follow a very precise and methodical protocol or maybe enact a whole antebellum cotillion fantasy, whatever. And if, at the moment, you're not able to articulate your sexual proclivities, your partner can conveniently refer to the bracelet. And it's got a default setting that simply says: "No wasted movement. No errant emotion. No extra tools."

MARK

Very nice.

JERRY

Now this over here is a terrific item for a child's bedroom, particularly if you have an adolescent or a teenager. This is an active-matrix color on-line mural. Basically, this is a five-foot-by-seven-foot electronic poster that's hooked into the Q-ratings of Marketing Evaluations, a company that measures the familiarity and popularity of celebrities and products. So the poster's image changes according to which celebrity is most popular for your child's particular demographic niche. Y'know, given a teenager's capricious tastes and flickering attention span, a parent can spend a fortune on posters. You can go from Bert and Ernie to Freddy Krueger to Troy Aikman to Shaquille O'Neal to Drew Barrymore to Snoop Doggy Dogg to Wyndham Lewis in a matter of weeks. With the electronic mural, the instant a pop icon's Q-ratings falter, the has-been is wiped into oblivion and replaced with the face du jour. And remember, the on-line poster is constantly analyzing your child's demographic profile as it evolves, so that . . . Mr. Leyner, would you excuse me for one second while I help that customer over there?

MARK

Hey, that's my old rabbi!

JERRY

Excuse me?

MARK

That's Rabbi Weiner, the rabbi who bar-mitzvahed me.

MARK *approaches the* RABBI.

MARK

Rabbi Weiner, you probably don't remember me . . .

RABBI

No, I'm sorry.

MARK

You bar-mitzvahed me in 1969—the year the Jets beat the Baltimore Colts in the Super Bowl, 16–7. Rabbi, at my bar mitzvah, you whispered something to me. You said, "Mark, I want you always to remember—" But your mouth was too close to my ear and whatever it was that you wanted me to always remember was completely unintelligible. And I've always had this nagging feeling that my life might have been very different had I understood what you said to me. I don't suppose you—

RABBI

(Shaking his head) I don't have a clue. I'm sorry. I wish I could say that I'd intended to leave you a garbled message, a sort of mystical riddle for you to work on unraveling for the rest of your life, but actually, after several similar complaints I learned not to put my mouth so close to people's ears when I whispered to them.

MARK

Rabbi, do you shop here frequently?

RABBI

Yes, I do. They have terrific stuff here.

MARK

Rabbi . . . you say you come here frequently, right? I know this is going to sound crazy but . . . You haven't ever heard rumors about Jews and extraterrestrials kidnapping gentiles who've defaulted on their charge accounts and turning them into little action figures underground here, have you?

RABBI

No. That's the most ludicrous thing I've ever heard.

MARK

That's what I was saying—

RABBI

We meet with the extraterrestrials down on Sub 40 on the third Thursday of every month. But we don't turn anyone into toys! We chitchat, we induct new members, we plan projects, we nosh a bit. It's more like a Rotary Club meeting. We've been gathering here for about 40 years. In fact, I'm here tonight for this month's meeting. I got here a little early so I thought I'd pick up a few things. I got a couple of pairs of those new Martin Marietta boxer shorts, and I'm looking for this Chinese medical exam table paper for my wife. She wants to reupholster the sofa in the living room.

JERRY
We've got that right here, sir. It comes in rolls of 200 feet—

MARK
Jews and extraterrestrials have been meeting under Bergdorf Goodman for 40 years? Rabbi, what are you talking about?

RABBI
Right after the Second World War, a delegation of extraterrestrials met secretly with Zionist leaders including David Ben-Gurion and Chaim Weizmann, leaders of the Irgun like Vladimir Jabotinsky and Menachem Begin, and several Jewish financiers—people like Baron de Rothschild and Bernard Baruch. And they proposed an alliance—a mutual assistance and strategic cooperation pact.

MARK
What kind of cooperation?

RABBI
Well, the extraterrestrials—we call them *Grays*—would primarily assist the Israeli military and also facilitate Jewish domination of the media in return for medical information—information about certain parts of the human brain.

MARK
What? What kind of information?

RABBI
They're very interested in the limbic system—that's the part of the brain that controls the fight or flight response, fear, rage, pleasure, that sort of thing. The Grays, as you

might imagine, are light years ahead in terms of ratiocinative ability, but their emotional development is a bit stunted.

MARK

And in return, what do they do for the Israeli military?

RABBI

Oh all sorts of things! Weapons research, surveillance, space espionage . . . It's an extremely close, synergistic relationship.

MARK

And no one knows about this? I mean the intelligence community, journalists . . .

RABBI

There have been UFO sightings for years connected with the pact. In 1945 there were sightings in Poland where some of the initial meetings took place. And there are sightings constantly in Israel, especially down in the Negev, near Dimona where the Israelis have their secret nuclear facilities. There's a huge Gray–Israeli Air Force clandestine facility in the Negev that's disguised as a desalinization plant. And there's major UFO activity there all the time. But no one's really put two and two together.

MARK

So no one really knows about any of this?

RABBI

Those who need to know know. Security is very good. A lot of the UFO activity around the world is really just a cover, a diversion. For instance, all the sightings out in Nevada at Groom Lake—y'know, Area 51 where U.S. military secret projects are built—that's all bullshit really. The Grays don't give the U.S. anything of importance, it's all purely diversionary.

MARK

And the Grays only help Jews and Israelis?

RABBI

No. There are some gentiles involved but they tend to be people who are very committed to the Israeli cause. And occasionally the Grays have offered technology to peripheral individuals or organizations, but there's usually a quid pro quo of some kind or another. Polymerase chain reaction; the abortion pill, RU-486; recombinant bovine somatotropin, the synthetic hormone that enables cows to produce more milk—that's all based on Gray technology. But the companies involved probably made fairly big donations to Israel to get it.

MARK

And once a month, under Bergdorf Goodman, there are meetings of Grays and Jews who are involved in this pact.

RABBI

As I said, we get together, we discuss the status of current projects, we induct new members—scientists, military people, volunteers for the limbic-system research—we eat. It's all quite innocent, really.

MARK

Rabbi, I'm standing here completely flabbergasted. You're

telling me that there's a 40-year-old, ongoing collusion between Jews and extraterrestrials. That in return for information about certain parts of the human brain, the extraterrestrials collaborate with the Israeli military. And that the principals involved meet every month under Bergdorf Goodman.

RABBI

Basically.

MARK

Rabbi, this is like the most vile, most paranoid anti-Semitic fantasy I've ever heard in my life. This is like the *Protocols of the Elders of Zion* as rewritten by Whitley Strieber. You have to be out of your fucking mind!

RABBI

(Leaning toward MARK and whispering in his ear.) Son, our worst fears about ourselves are often reflected in the vile prejudices of others, and often these prejudices are based on some slivers of truth, and our fears are confirmed. This can be very hard to deal with.

MARK *grabs the* RABBI *by the shoulders and begins to shake him.*

MARK

Y'know, I'm getting very frustrated with you, man.

TINA, *a fragrance model, approaches* MARK *and sprays him in the eyes with an atomizer.* MARK *falls to the ground, howling, writhing in agony. (*TINA *and* JERRY *kneel to assist* MARK.*)*

TINA

Oh, I'm so sorry, sir. I got you right in the eyes, didn't I? Jerry, get some water so we can wash this out of the gentleman's eyes, would you?

JERRY *exits.*

MARK

(Anguished, eyes tearing profusely.) What is that?

TINA

It's Bergdorf's own line of Pepper Defense Spray. It's a tincture of oleoresin of capsicum, which is manufactured from the resin of cayenne pepper. It's an extremely effective inflammatory agent. We carry it in a 5 oz. fogger, the 3 oz. atomizer, and a 1 oz. flacon.

JERRY *returns with water.*
MARK *rinses eyes.*

MARK

Hey, where'd the rabbi go?

JERRY

Excuse me, sir?

MARK

Rabbi Weiner. The guy I was talking to before.

JERRY

I'm sorry, Mr. Leyner, I didn't see any rabbi.

Something flutters lightly down through the air. MARK seizes it. It's a Blimpie's wrapper.

MARK

Merci!

JERRY

Excuse me, sir?

TINA

(Sotto voce to JERRY.) Maybe he's hungry. *(To MARK.)* Are you hungry, Mr. Leyner?

MARK

Now that you mention it, yeah. I suddenly feel as if I haven't eaten for days.

TINA

Why don't we go to the employee commissary down on Sub 26 and get a snack? My treat.

MARK

What about my daughter's Barbie bag?

JERRY

Mr. Leyner, go with Tina, have a bite to eat, relax, and I'll bring the bag down to you as soon as it comes in. All right?

MARK

OK.

★ ★ ★

Sub 26. Commissary.

SERVER

Good evening, sir. Would you prefer pastina or tapioca?

MARK

I'll have the tapioca.

TINA

Same for me.

The SERVER *hands* MARK *what appears to be a table leg and gives* TINA *what appears to be a teddy bear. At the end of the line, a woman seated behind a large bin of tools selects a hammer for* MARK *and an X-Acto knife for* TINA. MARK *and* TINA *sit down at a table.*

MARK

(Nonplussed.) What is this?

TINA

Go ahead, use the hammer. Crack open the table leg.

MARK *cracks open the table leg to discover that it's filled with thick sweet tapioca pudding. He tastes a spoonful.*

MARK

That's delicious! I've never seen it served this way before.

TINA

We get our tapioca from Brazil. That's where they grow the finest cassava—y'know, that's what they make tapioca from. Anyway, there was some sort of trade tiff between our government and Brazil where we said they weren't opening their markets to our . . . I think it was contact lens products—y'know, the saline solutions and the daily cleaners and the wetting and soaking solutions . . . Anyway, I think the manufacturers got together—your Bausch & Lombs, your Barnes-Hinds, your CIBA Visions—and they send a posse of their top honchos over to Washington and they sit down with the Secretary of Labor and say: "Look, Mr. Secretary, we've got an egregious case of unfair trade practices here and we've got to do something, we've got to start playing hardball with these assholes down in Brazil, y'know, we've got to squeeze their cojones a little bit." So the Secretary says: "Tapioca." Like just that one word. And the whole meeting goes silent, like "Yeah, that's it." So boom, we institute the Tapioca Tariff that makes it prohibitively expensive to export tapioca or any cassava-derived product to the U.S. Anyway— it's the same old story—when there's a market for a product, the producers find a way of satisfying the demand. So now we've got Brazilian tapioca smuggled into this country hidden in table legs, aluminum softball bats, soccer balls, CD-players, you name it. So Bergdorf Goodman gets its buyers down to the docks at the crack of dawn every morning and—long story short—we've got fresh Brazilian tapioca. Plus we're lucky enough to have Jean Casseau—who used to be the head chef over at Chacun à Son Goût—we've got him running the kitchen here at Bergdorf's—and Casseau's thinking is: Why not serve the tapioca in the containers it's smuggled in—y'know, what could be more authentic, more . . .

MARK
(Mouth full of tapioca.) Autochthonous.

A WAITRESS *comes by wielding two long fluted cannisters of MSG and kosher salt.*

WAITRESS
MSG or kosher salt?

MARK
No way.

TINA *slices open her teddy bear with the X-Acto knife.*

TINA
Oh, shit.

MARK
What's the matter?

TINA
They made a mistake. I got pastina. I'll be right back.

Enter JERRY.

JERRY
Mr. Leyner?

MARK
Oh, hi, Jerry. You have the bag?

JERRY
The bag's down in Toys.

MARK
Jerry! What the hell—

JERRY

Mr. Leyner, the Armani backpack-bag for Haute Barbie comes with a teeny-tiny little wallet, and apparently the wallet was down in Toys. But you have nothing to worry about, OK. I just spoke to Phyllis in Toys and I told her to hold on to the bag, to guard it with her life, and that you'd be right down.

MARK

I'm going right now. Where's the Toy Department?

JERRY

That would be Sub 39, Mr. Leyner.

Sub 39. Toy Department.

PHYLLIS

Here we go, Mr. Leyner. The Giorgio Armani backpack-bag for Haute Barbie.

MARK

Hallelujah! And there's supposed to be some kind of wallet in there?

PHYLLIS

That's right. Let me get it out for you. It's really quite adorable . . . Here it is.

MARK

Hey, that's really cute. *(He opens the wallet.)* They even put tiny photographs in here. You don't have a magnifying glass or a loupe, do you?

PHYLLIS

Sure. I assume they're just those stock photos, y'know, like the ones they put in picture frames.

MARK

Probably. But that's such a cute idea. Gaby's gonna love it. She adores little things like that—those tiny cans of Progresso soup they make for doll houses, stuff like that. *(PHYLLIS hands MARK a loupe, which he puts to his eye. He scrutinizes the photographs.)* Jesus Christ!

PHYLLIS

What's the matter, Mr. Leyner?

MARK

These are satellite intelligence photographs!

PHYLLIS

What?

MARK

These are computer-enhanced real-time images from photoreconnaissance spacecraft! *(Hands loupe and photos to PHYLLIS.)* Here. What do these look like to you?

PHYLLIS

I'm not really sure, Mr. Leyner.

MARK

C'mon, Phyllis. Take a good look.

PHYLLIS

Well, they do sort of look like digitized multicolor stereo-scopic photos from an imaging satellite—I'd say maybe the KH-12 or the SPOT—with a primary mirror on the order of, maybe, two meters, active optics, a shearing interfer-ometer, and a full array of charged-coupling devices and photomultipliers.

MARK

Exactly. And what about its orbit?

PHYLLIS

I'd say we're talking a 520-mile-high orbit and a 98-degree sun-synchronous inclination.

MARK

So you'd think from the resolution, right? But I have a strange feeling that these were taken from 22,300-mile geosynchronous range or beyond.

PHYLLIS

That's impossible. No one can do high-resolution pho-toreconnaissance from that distance.

MARK

That's not the weirdest thing. Look at the photographs.

PHYLLIS

I am.

MARK

Phyllis, look at who's *in* the photographs. It's me. They're all of me!

PHYLLIS

That's crazy. Why would there be satellite reconnaissance photographs of you in the wallet of a Barbie pocketbook?

MARK

I don't have the slightest idea.

PHYLLIS

What's this one?

MARK

Let me see. *(As* MARK *and* PHYLLIS *peruse the photos, they pass the loupe back and forth.)* That's me smoking cigarettes with Keith Richards at his manager's office up on Broadway and 57th St.

PHYLLIS

I thought that was Keith Richards. And what about these?

MARK

That's me coming out of the Dupont Plaza Metro Station in Washington, D.C.—I was covering the Clinton inauguration for the *Los Angeles Times Magazine*. And this one is also from the inauguration—it's me being introduced to Sigourney Weaver at the McLaughlin Group reception at the Madison Hotel.

PHYLLIS

And this?

MARK

That's me at the Chateau Marmont in Hollywood, writing "Tooth Imprints on a Corn Dog."

PHYLLIS
What about this one? You look so pensive.

MARK
That's me in my car trying to think of three foods with military ranks in their names while I wait for Merci to exchange one nursing bra for another.

PHYLLIS
What are you holding in this one?

MARK
That's a semen collection container. I was at a sperm bank in the Empire State Building.

PHYLLIS
And this?

MARK
That's me playing Chutes and Ladders with Lawrence Taylor at my agent Binky Urban's apartment.

PHYLLIS
And this one?

MARK
That's me talking to the Zeichner twins' attorney Susannah Levine outside the Trent Oaks County Administration Building.

Enter YOSSI *and* SIMCHA.

YOSSI

Mark, my name is Yossi Allon and this is Simcha Elazar.

They all shake hands.

MARK

You guys must be Mossad agents, right?

YOSSI

What makes you think we work for Mossad?

MARK

I just have a feeling. You are Mossad agents, aren't you?

YOSSI

I'm a Mossad operative, yes. Simcha works for LAKAM, the Science Liaison Bureau—it's a clandestine intelligence agency within the Israeli defense ministry. We'd like to chat with you for a little while. Would you mind coming downstairs with us?

MARK

Downstairs?

YOSSI

Just down to Sub 40, where we can talk quietly.

MARK

Well . . . all right.

YOSSI

Good. We're going to have to pat you down, for security purposes, OK?

MARK

OK. Y'know, Yossi, you look awfully familiar. You weren't, by any chance, at Mort Zuckerman's Planned Parenthood benefit in East Hampton last summer, were you?

YOSSI *shakes his head.* SIMCHA *frisks* MARK.

SIMCHA

You smell good.

MARK

Smell my ass. *(SIMCHA glares menacingly at MARK. MARK pulls his pants down and bends over.)* No, seriously, smell.

SIMCHA

(Sniffing.) Ummm . . . That *is* nice. What is it?

MARK

It's called "Duce." It's new from Gianfranco Petronio.

YOSSI

Gentlemen, are we ready?

MARK

Good-bye, Phyllis. Thanks for all your help. I really appreciate it.

YOSSI

Shalom, Phyllis.

YOSSI *and* SIMCHA *lead* MARK *offstage.*

After a moment, we hear a single muffled shot from a silenced Uzi.
There's a pause.

And then we hear celebratory bursts from several silenced
automatic weapons.
A splutter of soft thumps.
An eruption of dampened pops that—as the stage goes black—
dissolves into the mesmerizing sound of gnocchi falling into water.

hulk

couture

When I'm not crisscrossing the globe, honing my connoisseurship of the physical arts—an avocation that has
taken me from the fighting-cockroach parlors of Rangoon
and wet T-shirt contests at Khmer Rouge ruby mines to
the self-service drive-through liposuction emporia of Boca
Raton and Easter brunch with a self-mortification cult in
Montclair, New Jersey—I bodybuild. I'm a *buff* buff, one
might say. It all started years ago when I was working as a
junior copywriter for a foundering grommet manufacturer
in Jersey City and fell in love with this woman who'd
been hired to hum Muzak into the telephone for customers on hold. Spurning my clumsy cerebral advances in
a disabled freight elevator, she informed me that she liked
her boys beefy and well-marbled. Fortunately, God has
graced me with a protean physique and I've transformed 6
lbs. 7 oz. of mewling mush into 145 lbs. of mesomorphic

granite. So trust me, OK, I'm no neurasthenic dilettante—I'm All Beast, but a beast with style. I mean, you have to admit, it takes a certain panache to saunter into a crowded gym wearing a Nicole Miller cummerbund as a weight-lifting belt and then rack every station on the Nautilus circuit, right?

To my taste, the apotheosis of style as it relates to body-building is—and always will be—the penitentiary exercise yard: brutal sun, hot metal, big muscle, major ambient menace. The unadorned hardcore world of the anabolic mutant in stir. So if you want my expert advice, forget about the clothes. In the gym, sartorial contrivances are completely superfluous. Take all your iridescent spandex and Lycra fitness accessories to the nearest landfill and let the extraterrestrials use them as goalpost pennants in their rollerball tournaments when they excavate the ruins of our civilization. Bodybuilding style is articulated through a reductive medium—flesh on muscle. Traditional accoutrements are limited to tattoos, sweat, and body odor. Religious medals are acceptable if kept to a minimum. For amulets consisting of fur, desiccated flesh, or teeth, check house rules—usually posted at the gymnasium entrance. (I knew a guy who got thrown out of a gym for wearing his girlfriend's recently removed hydatiform mole that he'd had laminated and strung on fat gold-plated links—so take the time to peruse your venue's bylaws.) Bandanas are OK. But be careful. Most guys look like assholes in bandanas, like marooned cabin boys from the Love Boat. Some guys look real cool, e.g., eight-time Mr. Olympia and successful teletrainer Lee Haney; Japan's self-snuffing belletrist-cum-hunk, Yukio Mishima; etc.—but it's risky. A baseball cap's the safer bet if you insist on sporting millinery during workouts.

First up, what kinda body you lookin' for? A nice Bruce Lee—all sinew and tensile kineticism coiled up in your classic high-definition subcompact? Maybe you want a Lou Ferrigno—hypertrophic mass, hugeness, pure hulkocity. Here's a look I like, but it requires genetic pre-ordering, you can't get it off the rack—the Robert Mitchum or Sonny Liston look, the big strapping body that says: "I've never set foot in a gym and never intend to, but I can pick up this Subaru and throw it through your synagogue's stained-glass window so give me a double tequila and beer chaser *ahora,* baby." Just natural in-born bigness. Lazy barrel-chested truculence. Check out Mitchum in the original *Cape Fear* or a tape of Liston's brutal first-round knockout of Floyd Patterson in '62.

Once you've selected a body type, you'll need to choose a bodybuilding methodology. Personally, I advocate Lone Wolf Style. This means no trainer (you're both Dr. Frankenstein *and* the monster) and absolutely no spotter. I consider lifting weights with a spotter akin to trapezing with a safety net or cooking with pot holders. If you can't take a casserole dish out of the oven without wearing *little mitties*—c'mon, order takeout, babe. Same formula obtains in the gym: If you need a partner to help lift those *big mean weights*—sign up for yoga or CPR. When there's nothing to keep a barbell stacked with 375 lbs. of iron plates from collapsing onto your throat but your own two arms . . . well, if that doesn't get the ol' fight-or-flight response going, then nothing will. And when those arms begin to tremble with lactic-acid fatigue and your adrenal gland is gushing epinephrine and your heart starts pounding away—man oh man, that's bodybuilding in all its raw, epiphanic glory! Who needs the annoying and pricey exhortations of a personal trainer, when you've got the imminence of a crushed trachea to motivate that one last rep?

Do not pursue intellectual endeavors within the gym. This should be strictly verboten. Reading while exercising on a stair climber or treadmill—a sure sign of the fitness arriviste—is like wearing a Walkman while having sex. The brain's role in bodybuilding is primarily inhibitory and should be reduced as much as possible. (I model my workouts on the copulatory abandon of the headless male praying mantis.) Come to think of it, I'd stay off stair climbers and treadmills altogether. Aerobic exercise is vastly overrated; and I dare say, you get sufficient cardio-vascular benefit running from the fridge back to your couch to catch the *Haggar Wrinkle-Free Cottons Super Play of the Game* every Sunday to earn *some* comp time from the Grim Reaper—so don't worry about it.

Now imagine that you've achieved massive muscular development, chiseled definition, and perfect symmetry, and you're ogling yourself in the mirror one afternoon, and damn it if you don't decide then and there to write to the International Federation of Bodybuilding (IFBB) for information about how you can become a professional bodybuilding competitor. Let me save you time and postage with one simple word: depilation. The body hair has to go. The look that garners the trophies and, ulti-mately, the lucrative protein powder endorsements is Plucked and Basted. I recommend full body waxing. You're wrapped mummy-style from neck to ankles in a single continuous wax swath and then a board-certified depilatologist, grasping the end of the strip, "unfurls" you with the violent motion used to start outboard motors and launch gyroscopes. I personally find a full body wax more exhilarating than bungee-jumping, and, additionally, I think that it gives the skin a smoother and cleaner appearance than shaving.

If your bodybuilding and fitness regimen is directed more toward enhancing sexual desirability than winning contests, don't neglect your "olfactory style." Unfortunately, we've become such a visually oriented society that we—and bodybuilders in particular—tend to forget that the first thing a person often notices about you is your smell. Try a moderately gamey body odor, which says: "I'm undomesticated; I'm feral and exciting." Each morning and before I leave for any social function, I gargle with Johnnie Walker Black. I think that women like that tinge of hard liquor on a man's breath in the middle of the day—it contributes to that aura of insouciant menace that the '90s woman finds so alluring and so refreshing after a decade of male angst.

If you possess, as I do, a ductile physique—that is, a physique that's easily manipulated, that responds rapidly to component-specific weight training—you can customize your body so that it most appropriately suits whatever type of event is next on your social calendar. For instance, I was recently invited to attend the New York City Ballet Gala Ball at Lincoln Center. This is a black-tie affair comprised of a ballet program and then dinner and dancing. As I anticipated the event, I thought it probable that I'd doff my dinner jacket at the table, but chances seemed slim—barring some unforeseeable tryst—that I'd be dropping my trousers. So in the weeks preceding the gala, I put aside work on my quadriceps and calves, and went heavy on the pecs, lats, deltoids, biceps, triceps, and forearms—building colossal muscle mass in those areas that would be manifest when I took off the jacket. Worth the sweat? You should have seen the stunned expressions on the faces of tablemates Sandy Pittman, Bianca Jagger, and Heather Watts when I did my little prandial peel. Jaws dropped, forkfuls of beluga-filled blintz stalled in midair—total and absolute stupefaction.

Just last week, *Der Gummiknüppel*—the German equivalent of *Martha Stewart Living* but with more nudity and grisly crime—asked me to conduct a series of conjugal visits with Amy Fisher at the Bedford Hills Correctional Facility and write about it for an upcoming special issue. Now, this is an assignment that will require more explosive power in the legs, so I'll be bulking up my quads and calves with grueling hours of squats, leg presses, and calf raises. And because leg training is so strenuous and demanding, I'll be fueling my workouts with heaping bowls of Testosteroni, the Pasta for Men. For those of you who are serious about stylizing your bodies, I can't say enough about this remarkable and delicious fitness product— testis-shaped pasta made from the finest durum wheat semolina and enriched with natural steer androgens.

No discussion of bodybuilding and fitness would be complete without some mention of anabolic steroids. As the debate rages on within the bodybuilding community over whether contest judges themselves are encouraging the continued use of steroids by rewarding increasingly freakish muscle development, I offer the following advice: Be aware of the fashion consequences of pharmaceutical regimens. The use of anabolic steroids can cause gynecomastia—enlargement of the breasts in the male. If you still feel that the only way to remain competitive is to use "performance enhancing drugs" and if you do develop gynecomastia and intend to continue competing, I recommend Azzedine Alaïa's eyelet-edged white bra top for about $235. For warmth *and* style on the posing platform, try Chantal Thomass's ivory cable-knit bra for about $473. And finally, for those bodybuilders with gynecomastia on a budget, there's an adorable red-and-white checkered bra top by DKNY for only $50.

See you in the gym, big guy.

just happy
to see you,
chula

Mercedes is in the store exchanging one nursing bra for
   another and I'm waiting for her in the car.
My waiting game works like this:
   I have to think of three foods with military ranks in
   their names before Merci comes out with the new nurs-
   ing bra.
(The original nursing bra opened at the shoulder straps.
   My sister Chase told Merci that a nursing bra that opens
   between the breasts better facilitates public suckling.
   Ergo, Merci is exchanging the side-snap nursing bra for
   the center-clasp nursing bra at a maternity emporium
   called *Mothercare.*)
Merci's been in the store for five minutes and all I've
   thought of so far is: *General Tso's Chicken* and *Cap'n
   Crunch Cereal.*
I glance into the store and Merci's on line at the register.

This is a lucky break for me. Apparently there's a price difference between the side-snap nursing bra and the center-clasp nursing bra requiring Merci to either pay the difference or get cash back. Whatever the situation is, it affords me more time to come up with a third food with a military rank in its name.

Unfortunately, so far, I haven't been able to parlay this extra time into a third food. I've come up with *Beef Wellington* and *Caesar Salad,* but *Wellington* and *Caesar* are not military ranks but the names of historical military figures. I've also thought of *Kaiser Roll* and *Chicken à la King*—but again, no good—*Kaiser* and *King* are not military ranks but ranks of nobility.

Glancing back into the store, I see that Merci is now at the register. There's almost no time left and I'm very pessimistic about coming up with a third food. She's handing the cashier money. The cashier is refolding the center-clasp nursing bra into a fresh plastic bag emblazoned with the name *Mothercare.*

Who truly understands how the mind works?

Cognition is still something of a black box to neurobiologists.

What transpired along the neuronal circuitry of my prefrontal cortex? Just what happened within the network of excitatory and inhibitory synapses enabling neurotransmitters to alter the way that my pyramidal neurons integrated cortical signals across thousands of spines in their dendrites—so that suddenly (as Merci pushed through the revolving door and headed for my car) the words *Admiral Salt-Cod Fish Cakes* miraculously materialized in my consciousness?

Who will ever know?

Exquisitely sensitive to nuances in my verbal environment, perhaps hearing a child saying "Mira, mira" to his mother provided me with the phoneme that precipitated an instantaneous concatenation of lexical processing that resulted in *Ad-mi-ral* and then, in a cognitive flash, *Admiral Salt-Cod Fish Cakes* (a dish I once sampled at a diner in Gloucester, Massachusetts)—the third food with a military rank in its name, seconds before Merci's hand reached the car door.

Exulting, I pound the dashboard with my fist.

Merci looks at me like: What the hell?

And I'm like: Just happy to see you, chula.

bassinet mattress

day

The field is strewn with the recumbent, softly heaving bodies of the Chronic Fatigue Syndrome Research Institute's women's lacrosse team.

And a puff adder has coiled up in the web pouch of a lacrosse stick to eat its molted skin. (We call it *dermatophagy*.)

Elsewhere, a mêlée breaks out between people waiting on line at Sam Goody's to buy the director's cut on laser disk of *Malcolm X* and people waiting on line at Radio City Music Hall to purchase tickets for Kenny G.

And in Lake Tahoe, Angie Dickinson moistens a napkin with her own spit and wipes hardened tiramisu from the lips of a quadriplegic chimpanzee she's rescued from an NIH laboratory.

Meanwhile, I'm at Epcot at the Cedar Tavern Circa 1950 simulation, pounding down double scotches and arguing with a giant Jackson Pollock robot (hydraulic skeleton, latex skin) about the merits of my painting *Blue Ball*. Coincidental to the painting, but apropos of National Bassinet Mattress Day, I'm wearing baby blue.

The lacrosse girls ("like totally enervated") are now bright red, poached in their own sun-heated sweat. So Bubby, with the unctuous good looks and inexhaustible supply of peppermints, removes them with his fork-lift . . . one after the other.

When I was a little tyke growing up in the rough and tumble Greenville section of Jersey City, New Jersey—long before I'd developed my austere philosophy of beauty—I had a favorite album called *Bozo Goes Under the Sea*. This audio narrative, consisting of three yellow disks played at 78 rpm, chronicled the underwater adventures of our eponymous hero—buffoon by trade and benthic adventurer by avocation. Estimating conservatively, I must have listened to this album some 4,000,000 times.

At the end of the second disk, we find Bozo one thousand fathoms below the surface and in dire trouble. His oxygen has run out. He begs his juvenile listeners to "Please turn the record over and save me, I'm running out of air. Please, boys and girls, turn the record over! Turn the record over now!" he gurgles entreatingly. (Somehow flipping the record magically enables Bozo to obtain another oxygen tank.)

Hearing Bozo's asphyxial SOS, and like some skittish mom alerted to the distant puling of her neonate, I'd dash frantically to my Victrola from wherever I was in the house and, trembling with the exigency of the moment, invert the disk as if my *own* life depended on it.

And then one day I didn't. And I calibrate the advent of my maturation with that refusal—my first conscious immoral act. Bozo the Clown begged and I just sat there. "Let him drown," I snarled, sucking on a candy cigarette. I didn't stop listening to the record after that. In fact, I enjoyed the album more than ever, my appreciation now piquantly seasoned with *Schadenfreude*. There I'd sit, Bozo begging, me flipping him the bird and blowing imaginary smoke rings.

A couple of weeks ago my house was broken into and—in addition to cash, several guns, and some chemicals—the thieves took *Bozo Goes Under the Sea*. I was livid. Not only is the album an irreplaceable totem of my past, but I've been looking forward to introducing my child to its varied pleasures. (My girlfriend is due to give birth in a month.)

Because I'd caught a fleeting glimpse of one of the alleged perpetrators, I went down to the police station and was given several books of mug shots to skim. After several minutes of perusing faces, my task of trying to find the evanescent physiognomy I'd eyeballed was completely subsumed by a realization that swelled to a crescendo as I turned each plastic-coated page: These men and women—these assorted practitioners of larceny—were absolutely stunning! They were gorgeous! They seemed lit from within. Somehow their very criminality, their malfeasance, had imbued them with a vigor and joie de vivre that was radiant. Notwithstanding the lacerations, edemas, and hematomas they'd incurred resisting arrest, they were—each and every one of them—a unique paradigm of human beauty. It was the Allure of Immorality.

Wanting to corroborate this hypothesis with my own experience, I recalled various delinquent activities— shoplifting a suit, pistol-whipping someone in a bar, or, more recently, cracking an encryption system for E-mail so that I can harass my business enemies—and sure enough, I remembered, after each instance of illicit behavior, I'd rush to a mirror and stare at myself with utter amazement. The transformation would be breathtaking. I'd look dissipated by evil and yet utterly rejuvenated, vibrant—more sensual and beguiling than ever before! I exited the police station, lost in thought. Is it possible that committing an immoral act actually has a salutary cosmetic effect? Can it be clinically demonstrated that being bad can make you beautiful?

Now we're not talking here about the sullen, costive visage of the male model—the hooded eyes, the three-day stubble, the sneer—the look that makes you want to tackle the guy on the runway, hogtie him, get a funnel, and pump a quart of Metamucil into him. Nor is it my intention to explore the beltless pant, the laceless shoe, the hairless head—recent fashion appurtenances whose provenance is the penitentiary.

And we are accepting as axiomatic—without need for further analysis—the "ladies love outlaws" phenomenon. One need only consider that scene from *Bugsy* where Virginia Hill is reduced to a steaming puddle of liquefied G-spot by the sounds of paramour Benjamin "Don't Call Me

'Bugsy' " Siegel beating a business associate and forcing him to bark like a dog, squeal like a pig, and ululate like a Mongolian gibbon. Corporate America has been exploiting the "bad is beautiful" syndrome for years in its advertising campaigns, endlessly recycling its cast of eye-patched corsairs and brooding Heathcliffs to hawk product. In fact, I just visited the prestigious Madison Avenue advertising agency which is developing the television campaign for *Bastard*—the new men's fragrance derived from the pineal glands of death-row inmates. (In a commercial scheduled to air this fall, a woman is visiting her incarcerated boyfriend. There's a close-up of their hands poignantly aligned on the glass partition, as she whispers, "You bastard . . .") And thanks to fashion's much ballyhooed retro-swing, we may soon be seeing felonious waifs in bell-bottoms and Pez chokers.

The connection between crime and beauty is so profound and abiding that I've often wondered why condemned prisoners are permitted to choose their last meal, but not the outfit in which they're going to be executed. This sartorial deprivation seems not only cruel and unusual, but inimical to our culture's fascination with sociopathic fashion. Perhaps the "last-outfit prerogative" has not gained wide acceptance because it requires a level of connoisseurship that would slow the creaking wheels of justice even more: While a blistered crepe blouse embroidered with small mirrors and chiffon slacks the color of mulled wine might be perfect for the electric chair, it's just plain wrong for lethal injection, where a simple blazer and turtleneck works best, and so on.

The *allure of immorality* phenomenon, an element of which involves the aggrandizement of predation, is apparently not limited to our appreciation of the human species. The Dean of Student Affairs at an elite Ivy League university told me over the phone that instead of posters of cuddly puppies and kittens, today's freshman girl is more likely to emblazon her dorm-room walls with an enlarged photo of hyenas ravaging an antelope carcass or a python sucking down that last inch of gerbil tail. Is this all about wrongdoing? Or is it the thrill of Darwinian natural selection? Why was I so excited when my pregnant girlfriend informed me that not only didn't she want any anesthesia during labor, but that she would also refuse anesthesia even if she needed a C-section? Why is this sort of recalcitrant toughness so alluring?

This much we have established: Fashionable men are affecting something I call the "post-transgressive" look. This is the male corollary to the post-coital look (tousled hair, glazed eyes, runny mascara, etc.) that has traditionally been so popular for women. By post-transgressive, I mean the look of someone *after* the commission of the crime or immoral act. This is not the passionate contorted face of someone in flagrante delicto, but the cool, smug, sinister look of someone who's already done the deed. But whatever we call it, more and more men are realizing that immorality actually becomes them, as more and more women are admitting how libidinally stirring antisocial behavior is. (I've talked to numerous female friends and they all assert, with striking unanimity, that the bald post-transgressive Michael Milken is infinitely sexier than the toupeed Milken who insisted on his innocence.)

Which crimes imbue a person with sexiness and which do not? Although this is a matter of taste, and thus it's difficult to establish normative guidelines, I can assert with some confidence that crimes against humanity, environmental terrorism, swindling the handicapped, and matricide (although there are exceptions here) do not enhance the appearance. According to the experts whom I've spoken to, the crime that has the most salutary cosmetic effect on its perpetrator is intramural murder—one cartel member car-bombing another, a goombah garotting his pal, that sort of thing. There's no pity for the victim and the killer's ruthless ambition is apparently an ultra turn-on—or so confide my female informants.

OK, so we're dealing with a widespread and age-old phenomenon here. As Blake perceived the allure of Satan and his underboss Beelzebub fulminating in their infernal clubhouse in Milton's *Paradise Lost,* so did latter-day culture buffs appreciate the malevolent glamour of Gotti and Gravano scheming on the sidewalks of Little Italy. But to my rigorous sensibility, this is all still much too amorphous and theoretical. I'm a writer and aesthetician by trade, but an internist and surgeon by avocation. (Following step-by-step instructions from a Chinese urological journal, I recently reversed a friend's vasectomy. The guy had passed out after drinking a fifth of Glenfiddich while we watched a Knicks game on TV, and I couldn't refrain from availing myself of the opportunity to attempt the surgery. I'm pleased to report that the procedure was a complete success—my pal and his secretary just had twins!) I like my phenomena anatomized with the keen and ice-cold laser beam of logic.

So I set out to explore the allure of immorality by consulting one of the nation's leading experts, Dr. Basil Macpherson, former president of the Wilford Military Academy of Beauty and the present chairman of the Department of Forensic Cosmetology at the Community College of the Finger Lakes. What I learned from Dr. Macpherson shocked me.

According to Macpherson—who bolstered his assertions with a dizzying assortment of anatomical models, endoscopic videos, and satellite surveillance photographs—the scientific community and the U.S. government has known for quite some time that immoral behavior has a demonstrably rejuvenating effect on the human body.

"Along with many of my colleagues, I'd always had a gut feeling that delinquent behavior had to have an observable and quantifiable biochemical effect that made the individual more youthful, more handsome. Once we had access to the new imaging technology—the MRIs, the PET scans, the digital subtraction angiography—the whole field was revolutionized. We were able to scrutinize the neurochemical and endocrinological processes taking place in individuals who embezzled money from their companies or stole automobiles or habitually sired children out of wedlock, and we were able to finally determine that immoral behavior has an antioxidant effect—it precipitates a chain of reactions in the body that neutralizes free radicals, the metabolic byproducts that damage the cells and accelerate aging."

I was flabbergasted.

"Dr. Macpherson, are you saying that the government and the nation's scientific brain trust has known all along that criminal activity and unethical interpersonal behavior actually has a biochemically rejuvenating effect?"

"That's right."

"And they've—you've—suppressed this information?"

"Well, of course. What do you think would happen if word got out that running red lights and tax fraud and philandering and felonious assault can do more to make you look and feel younger than all the goddamn ginseng in China? I can tell you what would happen in two words: total anarchy."

Well, there you have it. Scientific proof of what we've suspected all along. Why do bad boys look so good? Because being bad is good for you. Now before you go running off to knock some old crone out of her wheelchair and snatch her purse, caveat emptor. Last month, word leaked out (excuse the expression) that scientists had isolated a compound called genistein from the urine of men who eat a traditional Japanese diet. (In test tubes, genistein blocks angiogenesis, the growth of new blood vessels that's essential for tumors to spread.) And health fanatics started guzzling the urine of Japanese men by the gallon. So I suggest that if you're not predisposed to larceny and interpersonal mayhem, wait for further research.

Now, many of the men I know covet that seductive combination of dissolute looks and youthful vigor that immoral behavior imparts, but they don't want to actually *be* immoral or dissolute. They've got families or jobs they won't jeopardize and they just can't afford to "act out."

"If only I could strike a kind of inverse Faustian bargain, do a sort of reverse Dorian Gray—where I could *look* evil without having to *be* evil," mused a friend who longs for psychopathic looks, but has two kids and a wife and can't commit the heinous deeds that would appropriately chisel his soul and his face. (In Oscar Wilde's *The Picture of Dorian Gray,* Dorian relinquishes his soul so that his portrait ages and he remains young, but the portrait ceases to mirror Dorian's external beauty, mirroring instead his internal ugliness—"he held the light up again to the canvas . . . through some strange quickening of inner life, the leprosies of sin were slowly eating the thing away.")

I'm a practical-minded guy, so I'll leave the inverse Faustian pacts to my more fanciful colleagues. But I can offer some advice to those of you who didn't enjoy the luxury of having been brought up in a criminal milieu— those of you who weren't dandled on the knees of extortionists and loan sharks, but who wish you looked like you were.

Plastic surgeons are increasingly offering their male patients a smorgasbord of procedures that enable them to look like they've been very bad. One prominent plastic surgeon told me about a patient—a CPA from Bethpage, Long Island—who wanted to look like Keith Richards, but who didn't smoke, didn't drink, didn't take drugs, and who was in bed every night by 10 P.M. with a warm Ovaltine. The doctor performed what's called a rhytiplasty, scoring the man's face with hundreds of wrinkles and crevices—giving him the gaunt, debauched appearance of a genuine Exile on Main Street.

I personally recommend a more hands-on, do-it-yourself approach. You're a nice, ethical, sensitive guy— trouble is, you've got a date with this wild bombshell and you want to look like a real Reservoir Dog. Not to worry. Get yourself a No. 3 scalpel handle and a No. 10 disposable scalpel blade. Two or three days before your date, make a few incisions on your face, preferably over the eyes and around the mouth. The healing lacerations and eventual scars say to women "I'm loco, you'll have a good time with me." When making the incisions, try to simulate randomness—think of Zen calligraphy—you don't want the cicatrization to seem contrived. If you want to get fancy, try wounds that require suturing. These can make for more interesting scars. I recommend nonabsorbable chromic gut sutures and a 2.5-cm tapered needle. And for those of you who are really ambitious, there are electro-surgical tools that feature cutting and coagulation currents.

Next, get yourself a pair of external defibrillation pad-dles. About fifteen minutes before you go to pick up your date, coat your chest with conductive cream and zap yourself with the defibrillator paddles. Nothing that I know of gives a man that manic, hell-bent appearance more effectively than 300 joules of electricity.

And don't forget that essential "I'm bad" fashion acces-sory—the electronic ankle bracelet, that simple yet elegant device that says "I'm a high-risk probationer under elec-tronically monitored house arrest."

And finally, one last bit of advice, a little tip I've never shared with anyone before. But what the hell, I can take the competition. When you're out with your date, flatter her perineum. It's a real original touch and it says "I'm an insouciant, devil-may-care, sleazy, 'let Bozo drown' kind of guy."

Sound crazy? Hey, it works for me.

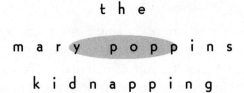

the
mary poppins
kidnapping

Parents of one of three teenage boys arrested for kidnapping and imprisoning a female English tourist in Teaneck, New Jersey, blame the film *Mary Poppins* for their son's misconduct.

"I rented the video for my son and his friends as an alternative to the violent filth they usually watch," said the mother, whose name is being withheld due to her son's age. "As the movie progressed, I could see that they were becoming really disturbed. By the end of the film, they were out of control, demanding a nanny in very threatening tones. When I told them that we couldn't afford a nanny, they ran out of the house—they were bonkers, they were very agitated at that point. I just don't think it's appropriate for movie companies and video stores to allow children to have access to movies like this, knowing that it causes this kind of behavior."

Arresting officer Sgt. Jason Barbet confirmed the fact that the three boys had viewed the movie: "The juvenile suspects said in separate interviews that they'd just finished watching *Mary Poppins*. They said the movie really made them want a nanny who would do things for them and intervene when their parents were angry with them." None of the three remembers the exact words, if any, that were spoken at the moment it was agreed upon to go out and "hunt nanny," but they all remember desiring an English woman, so they went to the public library because, according to what they told Sgt. Barbet, "That's where the English books are."

The thirty-eight-year-old English graphic designer, Hester Bonapace, was treated at and released from Holy Name Hospital in Teaneck. According to Teaneck police, the boys allegedly coerced Bonapace into accompanying them back to one of their homes and then forced her to sugar their medicine, recite doggerel exhorting them to clean their rooms, and to slide repeatedly down a wooden banister. A hospital spokesman confirmed that several large splinters were removed from Ms. Bonapace's buttocks.

Only one month ago, in an incident that's come to be known as the "Mr. French kidnapping," a gang of girls in Tampa, Florida, abducted a bearded Englishman after watching an episode of "Family Affair." In light of the Mr. French and *Mary Poppins* kidnappings, ABC has canceled its scheduled airing of *The Sound of Music*. Sociologist Janisse Schlossberg from the Community College of the Finger Lakes in Canandaigua, New York, applauds ABC's decision. "It's egregiously irresponsible to expose young people from middle- and low-income families to films depicting ostentatious affluence. It has the potential for provoking very explosive antisocial behavior. You have to be extremely naïve to say that if a group of urban youths watch *The Sound of Music* and then go off on a gazebo-defacing spree that there isn't clear and demonstrable causality."

Blockbuster Video has announced that it will affix labels on all movies depicting affluent and idyllic childhoods which will read: "Warning. This film may provoke class enmity and pathological envy in some younger viewers."

Michael Eisner, Walt Disney chairman, called the alleged link between *Mary Poppins* and the Teaneck kidnapping "an imaginative meringue whipped up by venal, publicity-seeking attorneys."

"Where were the parents?" Eisner asked. "Children shouldn't be allowed to watch a film like *Mary Poppins* unsupervised. The parents should be there to stop the video at various points and to engage their children in dialogue. Parents need to sit down with their children and discuss the fact that not every family can have a magical nanny."

Bowing slightly to growing pressure from parents groups and radio talk-show hosts, Eisner said that Disney was considering including a parental guidance pamphlet with each rental copy of *Mary Poppins*. "The gist of it is teaching parents how to teach their kids that, basically, if you stay in school, stay away from drugs, and use a condom, someday you might actually have a magical nanny."

"And," Eisner winked, "it also explains to parents how to teach kids that, in the event that they do prosper in life and are able to employ a magical nanny, that they be sure to make all the proper tax and FICA withholdings on nanny's salary."

the (illustrated) body politic

There are fascinating and eerie parallels between Arkady G. Bronnikov's study of convicts' tattoos in Russian gulags (which recently appeared on the *New York Times* Op-Ed page, excerpted from *Natural History* magazine) and my own investigation into the arcane world of tattooing in the United States Senate. Like the prisons and labor camps that Bronnikov researched, the U.S. Senate is an insular, predominantly male culture with a rigid hierarchy that is articulated through a byzantine and almost impenetrably encoded lexicon and iconography. Although the gulag tattoo is typically rendered in a lush, lurid pictorial style and the Senatorial tattoo tends to be minimalist—designed for optimal legibility like an Olympic mascot—both function as resumés of past deeds and as advertisements of the bearer's place in the institutional pecking order. Given the voyeuristic scrutiny applied to the life of a U.S. Senator, the fact that, until now, the subject of ritual tattooing has been so completely hidden from public view bespeaks the talismanic power invested in these pigmented images.

Obviously, Senators shun commercial tattoo parlors—they tattoo themselves and each other. Although, as in the gulag, the tattooing methods are primitive and painful, unlike their Russian counterparts, Senators do not consider the ability to withstand pain a sign of bravery—sour mash is the traditional anodyne. Careful viewing of C-SPAN broadcasts will occasionally yield the glimpse of a Senator feigning sleep as, beneath the overcoat draped across his lower trunk, an esteemed colleague applies the ink with any number of sharp instruments—a honed paperclip, tiepin, the nub of a pen. (Special status is accorded tattoos applied with pens that have been used to sign significant legislation into law—especially if that legislation brought some windfall to the Senator's state.)

Whereas Russian convicts are tattooed over the entirety of their bodies, including their faces and hands, Senators restrict their tattoos to their torsos, buttocks, and limbs. Only the upper portion of the arm is tattooed, enabling the Senator to pose with rolled-up shirt sleeves for the photo-op of him flipping burgers at a union barbecue or sparring in a senior-citizen tae kwon do class.

The meanings of some tattoos are easily apprehensible to the uninitiated. Powerful committee chairmen are usually adorned with crashing gavels, ball-peen or sledge hammers across their chests. If a committee chairman also has an egg tattooed on each knee, it says: "I kneel before no man, not even a President of my own party"—this can consequently translate to "no gays in the military" or "no NAFTA." The most common tattoo in the U.S. Senate is a red M&M candy on the buttocks. This signifies "Miscellaneous Malfeasance." A Möbius strip indicates a Senator who has served consecutive terms over at least two decades and who's considered a consummate Capitol Hill "old boy" and yet unabashedly campaigns for reelection as an "outsider."

A tattoo can be a sign to other Senators that its wearer has extracted a lucrative quid pro quo from the President during a closely contested legislative battle. For instance, a mermaid wearing a Washington Redskins helmet means "I've kept an obsolete naval base in my state from being closed." Often the tattoo is indicative of the Senator's debts and allegiances to campaign contributors. A cow with hypertrophic udders means: "I'm pals with the biotech industry." A water-skier skimming across the Pacific on two pieces of yellow-tail sushi means: "I'm free-trade and antitariff." A golfer hitting a ball out of a steaming pit of polenta or couscous advertises: "I'm open to the blandishments of foreign lobbyists." A golf bag bristling with Tomahawk missiles signifies a cozy relationship with defense contractors. A lawn jockey whose mouth is stuffed with cigars unmistakably announces that "I'm a procensorship racist in the pocket of the tobacco industry."

Frequently a tattoo is a sign of past misdeeds and contretemps. A bee wearing a kaffiyeh reminds one's peers that: "I've been stung by fake Arabs." The image of a student craning his neck to glimpse another student's quiz says: "I've plagiarized." The semiotics of the California Savings and Loan mogul Charles Keating's florid signature enclasped in a valentine heart are self-evident. Tattoos can even refer to the illicit behavior of a Senator's family. A DNA double helix attached to a ball and chain means: "My sibling is a convicted felon."

The paw is the traditional symbol of the sexual harasser. Within this category is a special hierarchy all its own. A skirt-chasing Senator will adorn himself with a dog paw, a fox paw, a lion paw, or a bear paw tattoo, depending on the longevity and frequency of his practice.

A hairy Coke can, a copy of *The Exorcist,* or the state seal of Pennsylvania indicates a habitual sexual-harassment apologist.

The lowest of the low in the Senate pyramid is the diary-keeper. There is more invective argot for this creature in the U.S. Senate than words for snow in the Eskimo vocabulary. A Senator who keeps a diary, either taped or written, is usually forcibly tattooed by other Senators with the image of a simpering weasel poaching itself in a boiling caldron, or a grinning teenager lying on the median line of a drag-racing strip.

Like a Russian convict, the Senator has almost nothing of his own. He is in the thrall of public opinion polls, buffeted by the vagaries of his constituency's moods, and in political hock to his financial backers. The only thing that really belongs to him is his flesh—the canvas upon which he paints the icons of his prestige and infamy.

Next week, don't miss my exposé of the bizarre body-piercing and scarification rituals in the Securities and Exchange Commission.

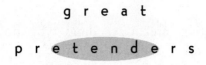

great
pretenders

Reports out of Mississauga, Ontario, a suburb of Toronto, tell of a real estate developer who is hiring actors and models to play happy homeowners at its Windermere Gate development, represent, I suspect, only the tip of the iceberg. There, actors and models waltz through living rooms, bake cookies and play backgammon, and sip espresso on verandas, their mountain bikes propped on railings, in an effort to portray Windermere Gate as a merry locus of genteel conviviality and aerobic leisure.

But surely this is not a lone, aberrant case of ingenious marketing. There's never just one cockroach, as they say. Look around—who else among us are actors or models impersonating the people we think they really are?

We inhabit a world of surrogates, poseurs, impersonators, double agents, undercover cops, placebos, bodysnatchers, and Stepford spouses. Who do you think those putative relatives are at weddings who don't seem to know either the groom's or the bride's family? Or those "guests" at parties who frantically stuff their mouths with canapes when asked to explain how they met their hosts? I'll tell you. Card-carrying Equity and Screen Actors Guild members, that's who.

What about that couple moaning orgasmically as they scarf down the pricey pabulum at some bistro of the moment; or those tautly ponytailed Amerasians accoutered in charcoal and black, sprawled sullenly across a Philippe Starck plumbing-fixture-as-love-seat in the lobby of any one of a number of fashionable hotels; or those audience members weeping and ululating inconsolably or laughing themselves into femoral artery hemorrhages at the coming attractions for a movie that's obviously headed for video release in the Punjab at the speed of light? Mercenary thespians one and all.

In all fairness, I must admit that I'm guilty of engaging in occasional recreational dissimulation, myself. Whereas some guys like to go off fly-fishing or spelunking or cuckolding Iowans, I like to catch some R and R by renting a small office in some sleepy southern town and posing as a dermatologist. Give me a week of excising cysts, incising carbuncles, chemabrading acne scars and lasering away spider veins, and I'm completely refreshed, revitalized—eager to plunge back into the slash-and-burn, eat-your-young, kill-'em-all-and-let-God-sort-'em-out battlegrounds of the New York literary scene.

So we need to acknowledge the ubiquity of dissemblance. Those deinstitutionalized gentlemen riding the subways in three-piece suits, "reading" inverted week-old newspapers in an effort to simulate commuting professionals, are merely more unabashed in their masquerade than most of us. Who hasn't made one of those wracked 3 A.M. self-admissions of fraudulence: "I'm not the savvy arbitrager that everyone thinks I am, I'm just good at pretending to be one" or "I'm not a good [Mom] [Dad] [Son] [Daughter] [Fill in the blank], it's all an act" or "If only people knew that beneath this facade of congeniality and generosity was a purulent misanthrope making do with 'Court TV' until the advent of televised executions." As a result of this epidemic dissimulation, we're incessantly urged by mental health professionals to be more "real." There's even a nice mercantile spin to the exhortation. "You've got to *own* your feelings," we're told. Well, given present market conditions, I choose to *lease* my feelings with an *option to buy.*

If dissembling is the pervasive mode of social and commercial intercourse today, what tactical countermoves are at our disposal?

Well, let's take the Windermere Gate case, for instance. I suggest that buyers' brokers hire their own actors to attend open-house showings and scour the units grumbling things like "Isn't that a termite egg?" or sniffing the air in the cellar and asking: "Is that mustard gas?" or to simply wander in and announce: "Hi, I live next door. As long as I take my medication, my compulsion to torture animals and set fires is pretty much under control." That should knock the asking price down a few thousand bucks.

Let's try another scenario. The mechanic at your auto dealership sticks his finger in your gush of pink transmission fluid, tastes, squints, ruminates, and then recommends an $8,600 series of gel-electrophoresis, molecular sieve chromatography, and polymerase chain reaction tests at a lab in Bethesda, Maryland, to determine the chemical constituents of the "unidentifiable" specimen. Surely you're dealing here with a hired thespian whose tool box is filled not with fuel-line wrenches and spark-plug cable pliers, but with head shots and this week's copy of *Backstage*. But you glumly get out your calligraphy brush and draw those fat round digits in sumi ink in your checkbook as this consummate ham FedExes a vial of transmission fluid to the NIH. Your chagrin is abject. And it's *not* the money. It's the conceptual disparity, the phenomenological one-upsmanship. It's his chess to your checkers. His nimble artifice to your plodding authenticity. Fight dissimulation with dissimulation. Go faux to faux! Rent a car for the day and bring *that* in. Or, better yet, go to another dealership, ask to test-drive a car (upscale dealerships allow you to sample their merchandise unchaperoned) and then bring *that* vehicle in to be serviced at your dealership. Pay whatever you're charged for whatever they do—$8,600 or $86,000. But you'll feel wonderful! Because now you're playing on the same board. Sure he's not a real mechanic—but it's not really your car! Check . . . Checkmate!

When I recently became convinced that my daughter Gabrielle's pediatrician was actually an actor playing the role of a pediatrician, I responded in kind. I hired a child actress and had *her* go in to be examined and inoculated. I crossed the proscenium and mounted the stage! I empowered myself by achieving conceptual parity.

If we all shift to the simulacrum, then the simulacrum, for all practical purposes, becomes the real. (I am violating a solemn blood oath I made at the age of eight. One night, several friends and I hiked to the old hydroelectric plant on the outskirts of town; we cut our fingers and pledged never to use any word associated with French deconstructionism, including "liminal," "endo-colonization," and "simulacrum." Sorry, boys.) We will all pretend to be who we are, we'll all be actors and actresses. Then, at some juncture, one of us who's, say, pretending to be fat, will decide to actually become fat in order to more effectively play that role. This will engender a mass movement from the simulacrum back to the real. This is sometimes called the "De Niro–ization" of culture. These migratory shifts back and forth from the real to the simulacrum will calibrate the rest of history. (It's particularly interesting to note rumors that De Niro intends to actually have his arms and legs hacked off in order to star in Jennifer Lynch's sequel to *Boxing Helena,* tentatively entitled *Shrink Wrapping Donald.*)

Speaking of Show Biz—what do you say you and I put on a Show? Well, maybe not a Show . . . but a play, a one-act, a masque. I own this really cool loft space that used to be a submarine propeller factory we could rehearse in . . . Well, I don't actually *own* it . . . But we could rent this loft space that used to be a submarine propeller factory. I took a look at it the other day at an open house. They had models impersonating actors rehearsing Strindberg's *The Dance of Death*—a tableau vivant version of the fake books they shelve in furniture showrooms.

You play the sophisticated, erudite reader—prosperous, well-traveled, tanned and fit—whose esemplastic (sorry, boys) apprehension of the text is an art form in and of itself.

I'll play the elegant, mordantly witty belletrist whose

writing combines the delicacy and voluptuousness of po-
etry with the rigor of science and the vivacity of jai alai.

All right?

Good.

OK. Quiet. Places everyone.

Now, from the top . . .

the

g o o d

s e e d

On the 71st floor of the Empire State Building, America's most elegant architectural phallus, is Idant Laboratories, America's largest sperm bank. If this seems just too good to be true—a delicious conceit concocted by Hollywood fantasy *machers,* perhaps—I suggest you take a stroll over to the iconic skyscraper on Fifth and 33rd. There, only a moment's elevator ride from the deco lobby, stored in Idant's customized rotary carousel system and kept at a hyperborean minus 321 degrees Fahrenheit in liquid nitrogen, are some 60,000 units of semen, each unit containing a minimum of 20 million motile sperm—enough jism to start your own civilization from scratch on some arcadian asteroid, given the availability of eggs and uteri, of course.

An aficionado of bodily fluids in general, I've been particularly interested in sperm ever since reading, as a youth, a *Dear Abby* column which described the quasi-immaculate fertilization of a girl who was impregnated by swimming in a pool into which some libidinally incontinent teen had just ejaculated. (One can imagine the clustered school of sperm, tails whipping the water into a froth, advancing toward the hapless girl's bikini crotch to that menacing musical leitmotif from *Jaws*.)

As the years passed, I grew to personally identify with sperm—the bullet-shaped head packed with genetic data, the midsection full of energy, the long posterior flagellum; forging with almost suicidal determination into channels of cervical mucus. I suppose I've always seen myself as, basically, a head brimming with information, an energetic midsection and a propulsive tail; delving intrepidly into the remotest regions of womandom. And I think that it's been these very spermatozoan qualities that have appealed to my girlfriends and wives over the years. I don't know . . . perhaps there's a special ontogeny-recapitulates-phylogeny allure to guys who emulate the plucky gamete.

Given my background, a pilgrimage to Idant Laboratories was essential. But I also think that any man whose corpora cavernosa has ever become engorged, any man who's ever sighed, groaned, and then produced the, on average, three milliliters of grayish-white viscous *elixir vitae,* owes it to himself to make the hajj.

Presiding over his more than 1,200,000,000,000 motile sperm, high above midtown Manhattan, is Idant medical director Dr. Joseph Feldschuh. Feldschuh—staid, prudent, knowledgeable, conservatively appareled in white lab coat and striped necktie—is precisely the sort of man in whose safekeeping you'd want your semen. A sperm banker's hours are long and hectic. Although it was well after 5 P.M., for the entire hour and a half that I chatted with Dr. Feldschuh, he was in perpetual *active* mode—

fielding phone calls, corroborating statistics, reviewing correspondence, glancing across his desk at a closed circuit monitor which affords him four views of his staff at work in various sectors of the lab.

As a writer, the notion of being paid to masturbate does not seem odd to me in the least. Still, there were two areas about which I was particularly curious. First, I was interested in the logistical aspects of sperm donation—the room, the magazines, the cup. Secondly, I wanted to know what would happen if a sperm sample fell seventy-one stories and struck a pedestrian below. Would the gravitational acceleration over that distance produce a lethal impact? What a terrible and yet quintessentially *New York* way to die—traumatic cerebral insemination. Unfortunately, there was a dour aspect to Dr. Feldschuh's demeanor that made it impossible for me to broach this matter.

But as Feldschuh detailed Idant's testing and quarantining procedures, there was one thing I gleaned right off the bat: If you're thinking of popping in for a quick diddle and $50 (the going rate for a sperm donation), forget about it. Idant is a pretty exclusive club. Prospective donors undergo a rigorous medical exam, medical history, and extensive testing. The criteria for acceptable donor semen are tough, with minimum cut-off levels for motility, morphology, count, and cryosurvival (not everyone's semen freezes satisfactorily, y'know). So, as a result of prescreening and specimen parameters, only about 15% of donor applicants are accepted. Chances are, guys, you and your sperm won't pass muster. But hundreds of applicants do—remember, this is the most extensive sperm reserve in the United States, and that means the most diverse. And for you gals looking to artificially inseminate yourselves, diversity is key. Idant donor profiles provide you with height, weight, eye and hair color, racial and ethnic background, religion, education, interests, hobbies, special skills, talents, etc. Say you're looking for a five-foot, Farsi-speaking, soil-chemistry major from Texas A&M, who digs Hummel collecting, skeet shooting and *osso buco,* and who's got a family history of pyromania, but *not* petit-mal seizures—well, you just might be in luck.

A couple of caveats are in order, though. I asked Feldschuh about donor motivation, and he speculated that the average donor is either interested in enhancing his income or in simply helping an infertile couple conceive. Well, consider the following: Do you really want the father of your child to be a guy who earns extra cash selling his semen? And how about a guy who considers his DNA God's gift to the gene pool? Who is this guy—some human puffball, wafting his precious spores across the fallow meadows of our species? Could be a real jerk. And since jerkism is probably hereditary—elegantly encoded in the base pairs of the double helix—the kid might be a jerk, too. And remember, even the best laid eugenic plan can go awry. You can pick a donor with Mensa membership going back to the Mayflower and a breakfront filled with gymnastics trophies, and end up giving birth to a slavering, brachiating moron. But it's precisely that aleatory aspect of heredity that makes Darwinian evolution such a crapshoot. So I say: Give it some thought, and then shake those dice and let 'em fly.

As our tête-à-tête wound down, I asked Dr. Feldschuh about the semen production process. "They masturbate," he explained succinctly. Magazines? "We have *Playboy*-type material," he said. (I have an acquaintance who donates periodically to a physician's sperm bank in Jersey.

"Playboy-type material" doesn't do it for this guy. He can only get off looking at Leni Riefenstahl's photos of cicatrized Nubians. So he lugs this ten-pound coffee-table book back and forth to the doctor's office each time. Chacun à son goût.)

Feldschuh escorted me through the facility. I took a quick peek in one of the sperm-production rooms. A small rectangle with a chair, a box of tissues, and a sign on the door asking donors not to take the magazines. Oh, and it's soundproof. I guess even veteran semen philanthropists can be real screamers.

As I toured the cryogenic storage area, I couldn't help but muse upon what the future may hold in store for the sperm bank industry. Given the inevitable advances in screening technology, I predict total decentralization. Perhaps sperm ATMs. Maybe even the availability of sperm in the frozen pharmaceutical section of your supermarket. Is it so far-fetched to imagine ovulating shoppers—their carts laden with produce, canned goods, and paper products—choosing from among containers of generic sperm (e.g., "Caucasian Big-10 School," "Homeboy," "Sephardic Jew," etc.) and higher-priced celebrity sperm, something along the lines of Paul Newman spaghetti sauce or Kenny Rogers roasted chicken?

Bidding the very gracious Dr. Feldschuh adieu, I reminded him that I hadn't yet seen one of the semen collection containers. Moments later, when one of his staff handed me the plain plastic jar with a screw-top lid, I could barely hide my disappointment. I suppose I was expecting an exotically molded and specially contoured rictus of some sort or another. Also, speaking as a strictly amateur "donor" and from a ballistics perspective, I couldn't exactly reconcile the angle of the erect penis and the muzzle velocity and trajectory of ejaculated semen with such a container. "Were you expecting something different?" the receptionist asked. "I guess I was," I replied wistfully.

The elevator ride to the lobby got me thinking about that small, dark, semen-production room again. The progeny of that claustrophobic onanism might someday date my daughter, clean my teeth, pilot my red-eye to the coast, quarterback the Giants, who knows . . .

In fact, if you're ever strolling in the vicinity of the Empire State Building, it might pique your experience of the city that day to entertain the possibility that 71 stories above your head, half the genetic material of the future President of the United States is being produced by some guy whacking off to *Rolling Stone*'s Janet Jackson cover for fifty bucks.

Oh, and to allay any anxiety you might have, there were no windows in the production rooms or in the cryogenic storage area, precluding any chance that errant semen—either fresh or frozen—might hit you in the head and kill you.

dream
girls
u s a

It's ridiculous to try to politically rectify the Miss America Pageant. The trouble with the pageant is not its political impropriety, but its spuriousness. The winner isn't the prettiest or the smartest or the most talented woman in America, so no one takes it seriously.

We need to take the Miss America Pageant very seriously. We need to take the notion of America's paragon of womanhood very seriously and come up with a contest that yields such a woman. Only then will we finally satisfy our culture's gnawing hunger for a queen. Americans have this chronic need for royalty, but we're intrinsically an egalitarian culture, and blood nobility is just too distasteful, so we prefer a kind of genetic meritocracy—that's where these beauty pageants come in. But the trouble is that pageant standards are ludicrously lax and the judges tend to be these infomercial hosts whose careers hang by such slender threads that the flatus of a fruit fly would waft them into oblivion.

First of all, the contest must be much longer in duration—I'm thinking of something along the lines of the Van Cliburn competition or the Olympic decathlon. It must be extremely grueling. And it must consist of events that will test contestants for those qualities that constitute our culture's notion of the ideal woman—a notion that is provisionally consensual and fluctuates with the zeitgeist, but that can be codified sufficiently each year for a meaningful pageant.

The consensus today is that a woman's cosmetic beauty is a trivial aspect of her value as a human being. But I submit that her health is not trivial—especially if she intends to represent our country as its exemplary woman. Miss America Pageant contestants should be tested medically on television. Instead of swimsuit competitions, I'd like to see MRI scans and colonoscopies live on the air. Let's take a look at what's actually *inside* our contestants. And if, as a culture, we agree that fertility is an attribute of our ideal woman, let's have board-certified gynecologists vet the contestants' child-bearing capabilities and render their judgments on a decimal scale with *ten* denoting the optimal capacity for a teeming brood.

Now, we scrap the other pageant competition segments (e.g., "evening gown," "talent," etc.), hire the nation's leading experts in their respective fields, and have them evaluate the contestants in events that meaningfully test their intelligence and skills. Just off the top of my head, here are several possibilities:

• Have the contestants simultaneously play chess with a Gary Kasparov or a Bobby Fischer, and let's see how they fare.

• Have each contestant design a simple addition to her home, and let someone like Frank Gehry or Robert Venturi judge their sketches.

• Have each contestant prove a particularly thorny mathematical theorem to the satisfaction of a computer "judge."

• With firearms becoming an essential accoutrement for the American woman, let's see how each contestant handles a LadySmith .357 Magnum—and let's get either celebrity gun aficionados (I'm thinking Wesley Snipes or Jose Canseco) or instructors from the FBI's training facility in Quantico to judge the competition.

• And let's do away, once and for all, with the vapid "How would you make the world a happier place?" Q & A. Let's sit the contestants down in front of a panel of Gauloises-puffing French deconstructionists and see how they do with some hardcore hyperintellectual give-and-take.

The winner—the new Miss America—should be the woman who has simply accumulated the most points in each of these events, so there's nothing subjective about the final outcome. Then we'd have our paradigmatic American woman, our Miss America. Strong, healthy, attractive, brilliant. And capable of helping add some biodiversity to the species' gene pool.

The following week, there should also be a corresponding pageant for men.

The respective winners should then be wed at the National Cathedral in Washington, D.C., crowned as titular heads of state, and installed in an opulent palazzo on an isolated mesa in Arizona. Every room in the palace should be constantly scanned by surveillance cameras, and there should be a 24-hour cable channel allowing us to watch the new Mr. and *Mrs.* America at any given moment on any given day for that entire year.

Now isn't that a vast improvement? Instead of a pageant that results in sending some professional ingenue out to grand-open Wal-Marts for a year, we've come up with a contest that not only satisfies our insatiable yen for a Darwinian nobility, but that accommodates our voyeurism for an entire year, while giving advertisers a rich new venue to exploit. That's good for business. And like it or not, my friends, that means it's good for America—Messrs. You and Me.

the making of
"tooth imprints on
a corn dog"

I've been commissioned by *Der Gummiknüppel* ("the German equivalent of *Martha Stewart Living* but with more nudity and grisly crime") to compose a poem for their ten-year anniversary issue. As I reported in the premiere issue of *Esquire Gentleman,* my first assignment for *Der Gummiknüppel* was to conduct a series of conjugal visits with Amy Fisher at the Bedford Hills Correctional Facility and to chronicle same.

The editors of *Der Gummiknüppel* have custom-ordered their poem with unusual specificity. The contract received by my agents at ICM stipulates "1,000 lines of free verse in the *poète maudit* tradition of Arthur Rimbaud, but infused with the ebullience and joie de vivre that made ABBA so popular in the 1970s." Not only are the stylistic requirements severe, but the deadline's a killer: They need the completed poem faxed to their offices in Baden-Baden in less than 35 hours.

This assignment, albeit lucrative, is no stroll through the park. It's not something I can bang out amidst the domestic maelstrom of pregnant girlfriends, ex-wives, codependent dogs, etc.

So I catch the red-eye to L.A.

I will hole up at the venerable Chateau Marmont in Hollywood—the hotel where the great Billy Wilder bivouacked in his youth—and I will confect my verse under ideal laboratory conditions.

What follows is 24 hours of the postmodern writer in vitro.

[Room 25, Chateau Marmont, 8221 Sunset Boulevard, Hollywood, California]

6 A.M.

A 22-year-old white male barred from competing in the 1993 Miss Black America contest claims to be a black female suffering from vitiligo (the skin disease that causes loss of pigmentation) and an acute hormone imbalance that's resulted in muscle bulk, hirsutism, and clitoral hypertrophy. Attorney Alan Dershowitz told correspondent Wolf Blitzer: "My client is an African-American woman with a dermatological disease and an endocrinologic disorder, and she's being quadruply discriminated against." Referring to Miss Black America Pageant organizers, Dershowitz said: "We will combat these cretinous hyenas in court and we will see them crushed like the filthy and obscene rats that they are."

In Phoenix, fifteen people were stabbed in a mêleé that broke out during a showing of the movie *Aladdin*.

And on Wall Street, Berlitz stock hits a new high after an extraterrestrial-alien warlord claims "monolingual humans taste better."

I have programmed the television in my bedroom to awaken me, and at six o'clock I'm roused by CNN. I mute the news and telephone room service for a sweetbreads burrito and a thermos of black coffee.

Several lines of verse have emerged intact from my hypnopompic state, and I scrawl them on a pad before they can evaporate:

> In a dressing room at Armani Kids,
> I found the dead body of a policewoman.
> I sucked her toe and she came to life.

There are also two fragments. The neo-Keatsian

> Beads of mercury dribble from
> the mouths of hemorrhaging androids . . .

and the evocative

> Tooth imprints on a corn dog.

After momentarily considering revising the initial lines to read: "At a counterfeit hair-care products lab, / I found the dead body of a policewoman. / I sucked her toe and she came to life," and then not (there's something so much more febrile and chthonic about discovering this sleeping-beauty-in-blue at a juvenile couturier), I decide against incorporating any of this material into the poem. "From the Mouths of Hemorrhaging Androids" and "Tooth Imprints on a Corn Dog" have possibilities as titles, though. (I also make a note to pitch the "comatose policewoman found in dressing room—protagonist sucks toe—policewoman's miraculously revived—becomes indebted to protagonist, who turns out to be the Vitiligo Killer" idea to a couple of movie producers while I'm in town.)

I stash the material that I've generated thus far in a safe in the bedroom closet. (I've taken rather elaborate security measures to ensure that no one plagiarizes my verse or disturbs me while I'm composing. The "workmen" who appear to busy themselves with maintenance and repairs in and around my suite are actually undercover security agents. For example, the "plumber" crouched beneath the kitchen sink, with the pants hanging low in the rear, exposing a good 2–3 inches of butt crack—he's one of my most highly decorated counterinsurgency operatives. The exposed area between the cheeks of his buttocks is actually *bugged* with hypersensitive microphones, a microcomponent electroencephalography device, a Doppler ultrasound transducer, and a remote telemetric sphygmoscope and galvanic skin response sensor so that he can record the voices, monitor the brain waves, image the internal organs, and evaluate the veracity of any person or persons who come within a two-mile radius of my hotel suite.)

Ravaging the sweetbreads burrito like a starved animal, I set up my Apple Macintosh PowerBook 180 on the dining room table, and I invoke my muse . . . my sullen muse in strapless black-lace bra, black-velvet short-shorts trimmed in fur, black fishnet stockings, quilted clogs and black *ET TU, BABE* cap.

And like the celebratory automatic-weapons fire of an anarchic mob, my neurons set the synaptic sky ablaze with electrical discharge.

7:10 A.M.

I am in ecstasy. Having donned an immaculately hand-tailored Savile Row suit, and furiously puffing True Menthols, I prowl my maze of rooms, entire stanzas of iridescent carnivalesque verse spontaneously crystalizing in my imagination. Elegiac overtures like: *A sensual, violent, good-looking woman in her forties, who drank heavily and was a recreational IV-drug user, my sister's torts professor captivated me from the moment I met her.* And tawdry, effervescent fugues like: *"Who the fuck are you, Hans Muslim Anderson?" snarled the Grissom gang's loathsome materfamilias from behind a lacquered shoji screen where she had loosened her chemise and was giving herself a crimson hickey on one of her enormous pock-marked breasts. Each of her fourteen-inch fingernails was a fastidiously manicured neon helix, requiring that even the most rudimentary tasks of personal grooming—from the daily application of her underarm deodorant to the topiary care of her bikini line—be performed by her strapping manservant, Patrick Ntambo, a cashiered ensign from the Ugandan Navy.*

These are among the gorgeous cadenzas I whistle as I clean the Augean stables of contemporary literature. My fingers appearing to evaporate in a vapor of speed over the keyboard of my laptop, I am slashing a path through the rank vegetation of American popular culture with the warped machete of my mind . . . all to the din of the latest *Chix with Dix* CD, whose turbid guitar noise sounds like a stethoscope's been put to the engine of a C-50 cargo transport, and which I play at such decibel levels that bus-boys exit my suite with blood oozing from their ears.

9:30 A.M.

Inner thoughts:

What a remarkable journey my life has been. I was born one of craniopagus quintuplets—five infants connected at the head, our bodies extending radially like flower petals. I was the only sibling to survive the surgery that separated us. My father was an imposing and remote figure, very much the martial patriarch who valued certainty and implacable resolve above all other attributes. (Father was particularly fastidious about language. I was with him on a plane once when he turned around in his seat and slapped a complete stranger across the face for mispronouncing the word *putsch*.) Mother, albeit not an intellectual—she was incapable of naming four American presidents, making change for $20, or reading a menu—was certainly a more empathetic and tender parent. But her influence was effectively muted by Father's strident and unyielding decrees. As a child, I was absolutely forbidden to express or inwardly harbor self-doubt. Soon after Mother's mysterious suicide, Father hired a telepathic governess from a Soviet parapsychology institute. If, in the sanctuary of my own bedroom, I had thoughts that even remotely hinted at irresolution or trepidation, the woman—an affectless martinet with an intricate circuitry of braids enveloping the back of her skull—would suddenly materialize to flay my bared buttocks with a heavy Cyrillic ruler, chiding in her eerie monotone: "Dun't sink negatif!"

After leaving home in 1972, I supported myself by

doing odd jobs. For twenty dollars, I'd arrange the cash in your wallet, President-side up in increasing denominations. That was standard. Specials included alphabetical arrangement by last name of Secretary of the Treasury, by ascending or descending serial number, etc. I did a job for a lady who liked her wallet arranged with wrinkled bills up front and crispy bills toward the back. A transit cop once hired me to arrange his bills by shade; this is called "the fade"—bright cash up front, bleached cash to the rear. *Chacun à son goût.* Specials were extra, of course. You'd be amazed at the things that people won't do for themselves, or can't do because they have their weird little phobias. A guy once called me—a young guy, I'd say about twenty-five—and he wanted me to cut up his expired credit cards. The guy had this morbid fear of credit cards once they've expired. Obviously there's some complex psychopathology involved here, but hey . . . When I arrived at the guy's house, there were two expired cards— an American Express and a Sunoco—lying in his bathtub where he'd flung them in a panic a week before. So acute was his aversion that he'd refused to go anywhere near the tub. I might add that the dude had cultivated quite a stench (which cost him an extra ten bucks; if you had really bad body odor, that would cost you an extra $10 no matter what I did for you). And when I picked up the cards and walked toward him, he recoiled in horror, weeping, falling to his knees, pleading with me not to come any closer. I diced the cards with a pair of shears from my tool belt, and, per our agreement, disposed of them in a landfill some ten miles out of town. I charged him $60—the regular $50 for cutting cards, plus the $10 surcharge because he stank so bad. Ironically, he paid with a Visa card—active, I assume. I also killed pets. (Pet "hits"

were a lucrative portion of my business. A lot of people wanted their pets dead because they'd become too much trouble, but they couldn't bring themselves to do it because they'd become so emotionally attached or for religious reasons or whatever—so, for a fee, I'd do it.) My first job, I garrotted an incontinent Schnauzer for a guy in Englewood, New Jersey. It got easier and easier after that. A woman once contracted me to kill her turtle. The lady's got something called purulent erythema serpens, which makes your skin look like Roquefort cheese, and she thinks she caught the disease somehow from the turtle, so she hates the turtle and wants it dead, and she wants to *see* it die. So I devise a nice little car bomb for the turtle—a matchbox pickup truck with a piece of lettuce in it and a cherry bomb under it. The turtle waddles onto the toy truck to eat the lettuce, I light the fuse, and boom! Arrivederci, Michelangelo. But I did all sorts of other things, too. I'd help you take your cowboy boots off—that was $3 a boot. If you were straightening a painting on the wall and you needed someone to stand across the room and tell you if it was level—that was $7 per painting, and I'd do four paintings for only $25. And I'd charge ten bucks to smell your milk—y'know, if you couldn't decide whether it was spoiled or not.

And today here I am at the Chateau Marmont—all expenses paid by *Der Gummiknüppel*—improvising a couple of pages of verse for more money than most people make in a year . . . the Chateau Marmont, where Howard Hughes satisfied his cravings for baby peas and young girls, where Diahann Carroll and Sidney Poitier trysted while filming *Porgy and Bess* . . .

What a strange, fascinating life it's been.

11 A.M.

I receive a call from Irene Webb, Vice President at ICM in Beverly Hills. There's trouble on the lot.

(It is now necessary to disclose that I've distorted the truth about why I'm in L.A. I've indicated that, having accepted the *Der Gummiknüppel* assignment, I flew to Los Angeles and checked into a suite at the Chateau Marmont to avail myself of the solitude and serenity needed to compose the commissioned poem. Eager to undergird my status as an incorruptible belletrist devoted to his art, I neglected to mention that I'd been planning to be in Hollywood anyway because production begins tomorrow on my movie. It's about a family that has a terrarium of tiny people. It's my original screenplay based on my original story which is based on my original eight-word haiku that I composed after an intravenous thiopental injection prior to my tonsillectomy when I was six. This is a Major Motion Picture. Mammoth budget, marquee stars, Oscar-winning director, lavish special effects, hip soundtrack—featuring *Chix with Dix* recorded at a higher speed to sound tiny. MAJOR.)

"What's up, Irene?"

"Mark, there's a bit of a problem on the set . . ."

"Irene, I can't hear it. I just don't have the . . . the mind space for it right now. You know I'm trying to finish this poem for *Der Gummiknüppel*."

"But Mark . . ."

"Listen, babe, first thing in the morning, as soon as I fax the poem in, I'll shoot down to the office. OK?"

"The trouble is that . . ."

"Irene, please!"

149

"All right, all right. Finish the poem. What's it called, anyway?"

"'Tooth Imprints on a Corn Dog.' Great title, huh? You wanna hear a stanza or two?"

"Mark, what I'd really like to do is talk to you about the—"

"Irene!!"

"All right, I'm sorry."

"This is the penultimate stanza of the fourth canto: *Tomorrow morning I am going to be eaten on 'The Today Show.' / Katie Couric will tenderize me with a rod used by 18th-century French nuns to flagellate recalcitrant convent girls. / And then, as Bryant Gumbel plays the drum solo from "Wipe Out" on bongos, / four factory-fresh Nissan Sentras—each towing one of my limbs, / and each driven by the respective MVP from Major League Baseball, the National Football League, the National Basketball Association, and the National Hockey League—will quarter me. / (The Nissans' odometers will be removed and put on permanent display at the Albright-Knox Museum in Buffalo.) / I will then be prepared arrosto in tegame—pan-roasted with garlic, rosemary, and white wine— by the Frugal Gourmet. / I am now being held in a combination green room / fattening pen where I am being force-fed tapioca pudding. / Directly upstairs, they are building the 'kitchen.' / I can hear the carpenters' footsteps, / the rasp of their spackling knives, / the unintelligible obbligato of their radios. / Strangely, I have never felt more serene. / I now understand impermanence / and I am one with the Void. / Is that the cry of a cicada I hear?*"

There's a long silence.

"Mark . . ." Irene says finally, her voice breaking.

"Yes?"

"Mark, it's stunning. There's a magisterial gravity, a lapidary beauty to the verse that privileges the reader to be alive at a time when you are writing. You've endowed Couric, Gumbel, and the Frugal Gourmet with an epic, almost Miltonian grandeur. The plangent call of the cicada is an epiphany, recalling Fujiwara No Teika, the great tanka poet and essayist of the Heian period. It's an astonishing achievement."

"Thanks, Irene. I'll see you tomorrow."

12:10 P.M.

The elation of an hour ago has collapsed into severe depression. I am wracked with doubts about "Tooth Imprints on a Corn Dog." Although I'm intellectually aware that this is a requisite pattern in my creative process—the alternating waves and troughs of euphoria and despair—the emotional pain is unmitigated. Convinced that the poem requires the inclusion of more anecdotal material, I comb my journals for suitable vignettes. I leaf through the battered diary that I kept during a period in my life when I suffered from canine acral lick dermatitis and spent my days licking, scratching, and biting at my own flanks. In stunted script interspersed with pictures, like some arcane rebus, I recorded in unflinching detail my descent, my season in hell. I drank anything containing alcohol. In fact, my bar was stocked with Sterno, Old Spice, Windex, Nyquil, Aqua Net, and Lysol. (Plus tonic, bitters, and pearl onions, of course.)

But this material is far too bleak and splenetic, and would vitiate the generally mirthful tone of the poem.

Perhaps I can somehow incorporate one of the stories I didn't get a chance to tell during my recent appearance on David Letterman's "Late Show," e.g., *I recently attend a garish tribute to the Italian fashion designer Gianni Versace (where I witness Diane Von Furstenberg's left breast fully emerge from her blouse—an event which, I've subsequently been told, traditionally signals the advent of autumn), and during dinner I'm regaling my tablemates with stories about my prior incarnation as a medical advertising copywriter, and I'm talking about how I wrote ads for a product called artificial saliva which was developed for people who suffer from something called chronic dry mouth, and I'm describing how the ad's body copy touted the product's pleasant taste and realistic viscosity, and I'm explaining to them how disappointed I was when the headlines I'd come up with were rejected by the client simply because they'd already been used ("Artificial Saliva—Don't Leave Home Without It" and "Artificial Saliva—Mmmm, Mmmm, Good!"), when this stunning and extraordinarily elegant Austrian countess whom I'm seated next to and who's been ignoring me through most of the meal suddenly turns to me and says in this husky sotto voce: "I'm very rich . . . and very bored." A remark which leaves me completely dumbstruck. Although for some inexplicable reason, I finally respond with: "Can your inner child come out and play?" Etc. Etc.*

But this material strikes me as egregiously blithe, posing a risk to the poem's magisterial gravity.

I am about to lose all hope, when a breeze wafts in from the open window. Actually, one can't even call it a breeze. Imagine an asthmatic fruit fly trying to blow out a birthday candle. That's the intensity of this wisp of a sigh, which conveys such a minute and evanescent concentrate of fragrances—first daffodils, then hyacinths, and finally lilac—that it might be more accurate to say that what's conveyed are the Platonic ideals of each fragrance, rather than the scents themselves. And somehow this most subtle stimulation of my olfactory nerve cells hits me with a force akin to that of a nightstick to the forehead. And the verse begins flowing anew.

12:55 P.M.

> The sky is perfectly white and veined with
>   vermicular trails of purple SCUD exhaust.
> In a go-go cage dangling from a 10-story construction crane,
> I am naked except for a 7-Eleven "Big Gulp" container
>   and a rubber band.
> "Swing me!" I call to the crane operator.
> I want what I've never wanted before:
>   terrifying centrifugal torque!
> "Swing me, gringo!"
> I laugh mirthlessly, eyes rolling,
>   never so profoundly convulsed.
> "Thanks, hon!" I wail.

The air is rent by a cacophonous peal of imbecilic laughter as a group of rickshaw pullers drinking contaminated home-brewed liquor beneath my balcony react to the verse that I have just recited—the opening stanza of the seventeenth canto.

1:30 P.M.

I telephone room service and order the 14-course lunch, including quail soup and steamed piglet.

2:25 P.M.

Nap.

6:05 P.M.

Russia is so desperate to earn hard currency, preserve jobs, and resuscitate a moribund economy that it's begun selling arms and military technology on Home Shopping Network. Viewers who tune in, unaware of this latest twist in the global weapons bazaar, may be shocked to see a svelte model in evening gown, pearls, and satin gloves caressing a Russian S-300 surface-to-air missile, as its price—$849.99—flashes in the lower left-hand corner of the screen. On-the-air callers are giddy with the incredible savings they're getting on individual weapons and entire weapons systems that up until now had been completely out of their price ranges. A housewife from Tullig, Arizona: "I can't believe it. I have three boys who all just graduated—two from high school and my oldest from college—and I just bought each of them the Kilo-class diesel-powered submarines you had on a little while ago. And I just can't believe the savings! Those submarines used to go for about $250 million each, but thanks to Home Shopping Network and the collapse of the Soviet Union, I got all three for only $2,250! And I'm thinking of getting the MIG-31 fighter plane for my nephew, who's being confirmed this spring. And for my husband, who loves cars and trucks and tractors—anything with a motor—I'm thinking, with Christmas coming, either the BTR-60 armored personnel carrier or the T-72 main battle tank. The discounts are just unbelievable!" Other former Soviet republics including Ukraine and Georgia have also lined up with Home Shopping Network to sell advanced fighter-interceptors, SU-27 fighter-bombers, MI-17 troop transport helicopters, aircraft carriers, as well as low-tech weapons like rifles, artillery, and ammunition. Home Shopping Network Vice President Beatrice Pinto told CNN correspondent Wolf Blitzer that their recent "Back-to-School Package," consisting of two shoulder-fired surface-to-air missiles, a dozen Kalashnikov assault rifles with five thousand rounds of ammunition, two antipersonnel cluster bombs, and a tank-piercing artillery shell, elicited the largest viewer call-in response in the network's history. "We liquidated our entire inventory on that particular offer in twelve minutes! People just seem to love the fact that they can purchase high-quality weapons and sophisticated delivery systems over the phone from the comfort of their own living rooms for outrageously low prices, without having to deal with shady arms brokers who ream you with exorbitant commissions and surcharges."

Luckily I'd programmed the television to awaken me at six, otherwise I might have slept through the night. What a succulent piglet! Kudos to Andre Balazs, Philip Truelove, and the entire staff here at the Marmont. I chase two 50-mg tablets of over-the-counter pseudoephedrine hydrochloride with a chilled Mountain Dew and return to my PowerBook upon which the embryonic final canto of "Tooth Imprints on a Corn Dog" glows in the Hollywood dusk.

7:30 P.M.

Inner thoughts:

This will not be the first occasion on which, shackled by inexorable time constraints and challenged to produce literature, I surface from the depths, Houdini-like, opus in hand. A number of years ago, pursuant to a large wager with noted publisher and incorrigible sporting woman Michelle Sidrane, I absconded to a villa at Roquebrune-Cap-Martin on the Côte d'Azur and, in a fortnight, completed a twelve-volume series of mystery novels collectively entitled *The Executioner's New Clothes,* which includes *The Executioner Wears a Leisure Suit, The Executioner Wears a Pinafore, The Executioner Wears a Habit, The Executioner Wears a Chemise, The Executioner Wears a Bikini, The Executioner Wears Jodhpurs,* and *The Executioner Wears an Iridescent Silk Chiffon Jeweled-Front Gown with Matching Cape.* You're probably familiar with the opening paragraphs from *The Executioner Wears a Truss,* as they've been widely anthologized. Note the cool, vibey sort of "Kansas afternoon" feel I achieve by juxtaposing madras, velvet, and terry:

> The two murderers have been on the road for almost fifteen weeks without steak au poivre, in desperately cold weather, wearing only madras slacks and turquoise chambray workshirts.
>
> Back in New York, the Executioner staggers drunk from the Four Seasons, lurching desultorily toward a white limousine. All postpunk ennui, he dives headfirst into the car as if into an empty pool. And he sleeps, paralyzed, face pressed against the velvet upholstery. Relentlessly, clumps of darkness devour him.
>
> When he regains consciousness, he's in a hotel room in Lake Tahoe. His girlfriend, Lucia, who's just emerged from the sauna, turbaned and swathed in

plush towels, is squeegeeing sweat from her face with the edge of a freckled forearm.

"Thirty thousand tons of New Zealand anthracite just don't vanish into thin air," she says.

"I'm not interested in New Zealand anthracite at the moment," the Executioner says, massaging his temples. "I want you to explain that dinner to me again—the one at your parents' house. You said it was some sort of ritual meal commemorating . . . what?"

"Many thousands of years ago, my people were forced to flee their homeland suddenly one morning. When they fled, all they had time to take with them were half-filled cups of cold black coffee, cheese danish, and the sports section of the newspaper. And they barely had time to get even one sock on. That's why each year, when we commemorate our exodus, we eat these ritual foods—the cold black coffee and the cheese danish—and we read from a special sports section, and we wear a single sock. On all other nights we wear a pair of socks, but on this night we wear only one."

"Oh yeah," says the Executioner, fidgeting with his genetically engineered superfeminine gerbils who stand on their hind legs and, grasping the bars of the cage with their front claws, bombastically shout "Egöiste!"

Meanwhile, two coruscating gold-capped buckteeth sprout from the holographic moon, as the tectonic throb of Hong Kong's subterranean synthetic drum machine rattles the city, and handsome triad gangsters who pomade their hair with their own semen and tote bowling bags containing the severed heads of their business adversaries sprawl in chic hotel-lobby banquettes made of molded whale intestine filled with thermostatically modulated runny Camembert.

10:45 P.M.

The final stanza of the final canto. It must be a concise, allusive, unifying summation of the disparate themes and leitmotifs of the poem, an intricate précis, an envoi; in structure—a perfect miniature of the work's massive architecture, in tone—an effervescent exaltation of life itself.

I'm working two veins simultaneously.

I've been exploring the notion of educational foods. Specifically, is it possible to utilize soup as a pedagogical tool? Essentially, what *is* soup? I ask myself. A liquid food with a meat, fish, or vegetable stock as a base and often containing pieces of solid food. And then it hits me—why, of course—soup is the ideal gastronomic medium for educating children about maritime disasters and naval battles. For example: Chicken broth with little macaroni Titanics and macaroni icebergs. Or Hearty Home-Style Battle of Trafalgar Bisque with barley Lord Nelsons. Defeat of the Spanish Armada Gazpacho. Cream of Andrea Doria. Battle of Midway Miso Soup with tofu aircraft carriers and kamikaze crackers.

At the same time, I'm exploring the lyrical possibilities of the 900-number tête-a-tête:

"Describe yourself to me."

"I'm a peroxide-blond in a black velvet miniskirt, actually."

"Describe something sexy that you've done recently."

"Something that I did that someone else thought was sexy or something that I thought was sexy?"

"Something you did that you found sexy."

"I didn't lick all the potato salad off my spoon before using it to stir my tea."

"Oh . . . that's good. Say that again."

"I didn't lick all the—"

"Slower."

"I . . . didn't . . . lick . . . all . . . the . . . potato . . . salad . . . off . . . my . . . spoon . . . before . . . using . . . it . . . to . . . stir . . . my . . . tea."

Now, how to hybridize these two strains—the pedagogical soups and the erotic phone conversation—into the germ of a final stanza, that's the problem. And then it hits me—why, of course—a sex-talk breakfast cereal with male and female marshmallow bits each containing an edible, lactose-activated, voice-synthesizing microchip so that when you pour on the milk and put your ear close to the bowl, you hear, for instance, one marshmallow murmur: "Please say it. Since Clinton was impeached, it's the only way I can . . . function. Say it slowly." And then another marshmallow responds: "All right, baby. I . . . didn't . . . lick . . . all . . . the . . . potato . . . salad . . . off . . . my . . . spoon . . . before . . . using . . . it . . . to . . . stir . . . my . . . tea."

1:15 A.M.

I've decided to forgo incorporating this material into the final stanza of the final canto. There's too much pathos in pornographic breakfast cereal. Now I'm just thinking out loud here, but how about something like: *As cyanide pellets are dropped into the bowl of sulfuric acid beneath my chair, / I*

extend the middle fingers of both hands. / "Fuck you all," I sneer. / I inhale deeply, and then nonchalantly blow a series of thick, perfectly formed smoke rings of poison gas. / Then suddenly my attorney appears. / "Here is my Magic Legal Pad," he says. / "Stand on it and it will fly you wherever you want to go—the Maldives, Mauritius, Tortuga, wherever. / And it's sanitary—after each person uses it, he or she discards the top sheet, so the next user can stand on a completely clean page."

No . . . that's no good.

I need something august. Something resplendent. Something like:

> I inhabit vast pavilions whose emptiness
> is set ablaze by the vermillion sunset . . .

1:16 A.M.

I inhabit vast pavilions whose emptiness / is set ablaze by the vermillion sunset.

Hmmmmmmmm.

I inhabit vast pavilions whose emptiness / is set ablaze by the vermillion sunset.

That works for me.

There's a majestic plenitude to it. A fanatical lucidity. A still, immaculate violence. A sort of ironic, elephantine, paradisiacal hegemony.

1:17 A.M.

Deep sleep, with intermittent drooling and spasmodic leg movement, and incremental hair and nail growth.

6 A.M.

[*Animated graphic of flipping alphabetical cards from Rolodex, indicating the myriad celebrities who've appeared on the show: Asner, Beatty, Cher, Dahmer, Eastwood, Fonda, Gotti, Hammer, Iacocca, etc. Cut to live shot of applauding audience. Cut to close-up of host.*]

—We're back with Dr. Étienne Ducasse, who says that because of the expansion of continental ice sheets, this may well be our last summer. Dr. Ducasse, along with colleagues at the Institute for Advanced Cybernetic Studies in La Jolla, California, has developed an instrumented skintight bodysuit with instrumented gloves and head-mounted stereoscopic display that will allow you to interact with a computer-generated summer environment. Some are calling it "virtual summer." Dr. Ducasse says that you'll be able to "experience" everything from surfing the Pipeline at Waikiki to prickly heat and sunlight-induced basal cell carcinomas—without leaving the comfort and security of your couch.

Joyce from Lake Little Lake, New York—you're on the air.

—Hello?

—Joyce, turn the volume on your TV down.

—OK . . . I've been trying to get through since Monday, so before I ask my question for Dr. Ducasse, I'd like to respond to the people you've had on this past week. On Monday you had on the woman who found that poor little creature "Winnie" on the highway and then hid it in her lover's nail salon, where it died. I just wanted to say: How could she? So she didn't know what it was. She could have called a scientist from the local community college to come over and take a look at it. She says she tried to call the college, but the line was busy . . . well c'mon, dial again, for God's sake! We get mad in this country at folks who leave their children in dumpsters and blow up department stores and what all—but hey, are we any better if this is the way we treat a visitor from another world? She says it died of malnutrition but it's not her fault because she served it food and it just wouldn't eat. Well it doesn't take a Nobel lariat to know that different planets have different eating customs and what's one creature's staple is another's poison. You can kill a black man by giving him a fish egg. One little egg—dead. Orientals can't eat frozen yogurt. To them its like the equivalent of strychnine. One small cup of frozen yogurt killed those six Chinese cheerleaders at MIT in 1991. So if you gave Colin Powell a big bowl of caviar or Reverend Moon a scoop of frozen yogurt on a cone, and then said: well, I fed him but he wouldn't eat—c'mon, that doesn't exculpate anyone. Then on Tuesday you had that entomologist who came on with the Twinkie-sized cockroaches from Madagascar and toward the end of the show she said that once when she was a teenager she hadn't been allowed in her synagogue because she was menstruating and how this made her aware of the misogynistic bigotry within her own faith and I just wondered if that could have had anything to do with sharks because I know from a trip my husband and I once took to Hawaii that they advise women to stay out of the water if they're bleeding or menstruating because that might attract sharks and they also say to avoid wearing any shiny jewelry that might look like the scales of a prey fish and I know that some Jewish women have a custom of wearing shiny jewelry when they pray . . . so I think her synagogue might have just been taking necessary safety precautions and I thought her criticisms bordered on anti-Semitism. And on

162

Wednesday you had the psychic who can locate shoppers' cars in mall parking lots by placing their ignition
keys under her tongue and she predicted that by the
year 2000 the Bloods and the Crips would replace the
Democrats and the Republicans as the major political
parties and I just wondered if she thought that in the
future Israel might mistakenly nuke Graceland and then
agree to pay reparations after Lisa Marie addressed the
Knesset? And yesterday you had the psychotherapist
who said that over time couples become inured to each
other's warning signals and I just wanted to say that my
husband and I have been married for 28 years and recently I woke up one Sunday morning and asked him
what he'd like to do that day and he said he wanted a
fat greasy egg roll, half-a-dozen polyethylene packets of
duck sauce, a fifth of Scotch, a pack of Newports,
Mahler's Eighth Symphony on the Walkman, and a
languorous baby-oil handjob from a Filipino X-ray
technician wearing only her lead apron. And he'd
never spoken to me like that before—I never even
knew he liked egg rolls or Mahler. So I just wanted to
say that you have to keep your eyes open because there
are very obvious signs of trouble in a relationship but
you have to catch them early. Now, I want to say that
your guest this morning, Dr. Ducasse, is very informa-
tive and I'd like to know if he thinks that my husband
and I should have any money in high yield international monetary funds and also I'd like his opinion on
tax-deferred annuities.

6:10 A.M.

I was apparently so exhausted last night after composing
the first two lines of the final stanza that I don't even re-

member having programmed the television to awaken me this morning.

I dial room service from bed.

"This is Leyner in Room 25. Let me start with a large tamarind juice. Are the Galápagos turtle eggs fresh? Then give me three shirred Galápagos turtle eggs with a side order of manioc curly-fries and . . . are the *sugared lard balls in absinthe* chilled? Yes I would, thank you. And a large thermos of black coffee."

6:50 A.M.

The phone rings. It's my sister Chase.

"Mark, I'm sorry to bother you, but Daddy's test results just came back. He's definitely got Hoover-Klebs disease. I'm on the other line with a specialist at Mt. Sinai right now. Do you want to talk to him?"

(Hoover-Klebs disease is a debilitating and fatal illness which, in its tertiary stage, results in the complete liquefaction of the brain, the viscous cerebral fluid actually draining into the paranasal sinuses. Death typically occurs in a paroxysm of expectoration. I'd given my father a home Hoover-Klebs testing kit for Christmas—this is an easy-to-perform, three-minute assay that detects the presence of the neurotransmitter acetylcholine in paranasal mucus. When he got a positive result on the home kit, he was hospitalized for more extensive and definitive tests.)

"Mark . . . do you want to talk to the doctor?"

"Chase, I'm about to craft the culminating measures of 'Tooth Imprints on a Corn Dog.' This is an extremely critical moment in the creative process and I will not allow myself to be distracted by anything extraneous to the poem. Do you understand?"

"Well, what do I do with Daddy?"

"Does he have his Game Boy and food pellets?"

"Yes."

"That should keep him occupied. I'll be back in New York in a couple of days."

8:00 A.M.

Call it divine afflatus. Call it esemplastic power. Cite Coleridge awakening from his deep reverie, the magical lines of "Kubla Khan" still limpid in his mind; or Shelley who, brooding in a wood that skirts the Arno near Florence, was inspired by tempestuous gusts to compose the interlacing tercets and couplets of "Ode to the West Wind." I was applying benzamycin gel to a rash I'd developed after attending The McLaughlin Group Inaugural Reception in Washington, when it came to me—the final stanza of the final canto—verbatim, end-stops and enjambments intact; the original two lines efflorescing spontaneously into sixteen:

I inhabit vast pavilions whose emptiness
is set ablaze by the vermillion sunset.
My menagerie of shaved animals is not open to the public.
But you may go to the special room
where every object is coated with Vaseline
and you may put something up your ass.
I will be down in half an hour.
Presently I am drugged and supine in my lichen-covered bathtub,

dazedly eating lichee-nut fondue
from a chafing dish of gurgling white chocolate at tub-side,
as a succession of anatomical freaks mount a klieg-lit proscenium
and perform for my entertainment.
A scorched breeze conveys the acridity of spent rocket fuel from
a launched garbage barge heading for the vast necropolis on Pluto,
loaded with the compacted corpses of executed insurgents.
It doesn't get much better than this.

9:15 A.M.

I've just faxed the 1,257 lines of "Tooth Imprints on a Corn Dog" to *Der Gummiknüppel* in Baden-Baden.

I'm in my customized, four-wheel-drive, All-Terrain Lincoln Town Car, heading west on Wilshire Boulevard into Beverly Hills, and I'm on the line with Irene Webb at ICM, and, as a peripheral slurry of pink and aquamarine flies by, I'm screaming into the car phone: "What do you mean De Niro won't get in the terrarium?!"

It doesn't get much better, indeed.

thoughts while listening to mahler in the afternoon

Last night after dinner, Merci (a Catholic) and I (a Jew) were sitting on the sofa reading sections of the newspaper. The television was on, volume moderately low so we could hear the baby monitor. Gabrielle was asleep in her room downstairs. In all respects, a fairly typical evening.

At some point, apropos of nothing in particular, I asked Merci how much longer she thought I'd live.

She looked up from the paper. "Thirty-eight more years," she replied, and then returned to her article.

I did the addition in my head. That would make me 76 years old when I die, I thought to myself, and then resumed my reading, giving the matter no further thought.

But this afternoon, as I listen to the rich liederlike figurations of the first movement of Mahler's Ninth Symphony, I wonder how Merci could answer with such perfunctory exactness. Notice how shorn of equivocation her answer is—no "about" or "some" or "a good . . . or so." None of the affectionate disdain that one might expect from a loved one, e.g., "What a ridiculous question, you have your whole life ahead of you, sweetheart!" No inquiries as to my health or what might have prompted such a question.

Just that phlegmatic, succinct, chillingly precise response: "Thirty-eight more years."

One could ascribe, I suppose, the certitude of her answer to her familiarity with actuarial tables—Merci works in the health and life department of The Owens Group, an insurance agency in Englewood Cliffs, New Jersey.

Or one could interpret her seemingly offhand remark as an oracular pronouncement made in some sort of spontaneously induced trance—although Merci has not manifested clairvoyant powers heretofore.

Or—and it's this possibility that disturbs me the most, as the long drawn-out coda of nostalgic resignation closes the symphony's final movement in D-flat major—one could discern, in Merci's certainty, a diabolically patient premeditation.

How typical of Merci's personality—self-motivated yet insouciant—that she would plan to kill me, but not for 38 years.

Perhaps it would be sad to live with the knowledge that my mortality had been so inevitably determined. Yet what would Gustav Mahler—a Viennese Jew who converted to Catholicism so he'd be eligible at the Imperial Opera and who only lived for fifty-one years—not have given for an extra twenty-five?

YOU CAN'T SWAGGER IN A SNUGLI

Ever since Adam begat Cain who (after he 187'd his little brother and moved to East Eden) begat Enoch who begat Irad who begat Mehujael who begat Methushael, thus precipitating a firestorm of fecundity that led inexorably through the millennia to the birth of my daughter, Gabrielle, man has grappled with the dilemma of how to be a good father without losing his *edge,* his *wild style*— that aura of danger and delinquency that's such an indispensable constituent of a man's sex appeal.

When the new father descends into the sulfur of his private laboratory to reinvent his public persona, the task of balancing the sweetness of his paternity with the pungency of the seed-spilling rogue who cuts a swath through the demimonde as he thumbs his nose at the grim reaper is a perplexing one. It's hard to thumb your nose at the grim reaper with one hand while you're massaging the gums of your mewling teether with the other.

As guidance counselors at East Eden Junior High undoubtedly admonished Cain and his progeny: "Making a baby doesn't make you a man; determining how that baby can function as a stylistic complement to your self-image *does*." Now, if you find this notion of infant-as-fashion-accessory repugnant, all I can say is: Check out the science, dude. Testosterone levels in the sputum samples of new fathers who describe themselves as "nurturing parents" plummet to about three nanograms per deciliter— that's somewhere between the levels of testosterone found in the spit of ministers and women. Scientists speculate that—in the absence of strong countermeasures—hyper-nurturing leads almost inevitably to a condition they call *hyposwaggering*. (As this issue of *Esquire Gentleman* goes to press, neuroscientists at the National Institute of Mental Health neurophysiology lab in Poolesville, Maryland, have established a link between the brain hormone vasopressin and monogamy, parenting, and hyposwaggering in the male prairie vole.)

Be it subtly, debonairly, ostentatiously, raucously, or downright obstreperously—a man's gotta swagger. In 1894—the same year that British physicist Osborne Reynolds revolutionized the study of fluid dynamics by defining *mixing* as "the stretching and folding of a material," Heinrich Münze, fashion columnist for the Prussian gazette and rotogravure *Herrschaft,* anatomized *swagger* as "truculence flanged with irony and an insouciance in the face of death."

I submit to you, gentlemen, that it is not physically possible to swagger with a sleeping pink papoose slung from your chest. You can't swagger in a Snugli.

A VESTIGIAL NIMBUS OF AFTERSHAVE

"But surely there's a way that I can be a good and caring father without having to relinquish that berserk, in-your-face, icon-smashing, debauched demeanor that I've worked so assiduously to cultivate?"

Yes, friend, there is a way. But it's going to require a serious commitment on your part. It's never been as problematical to do the daddy thing while maintaining one's Heathcliffian side—one's joie de machismo—as it is today.

It wasn't so long ago when the more egregiously inept you were as a father the more alluring you were to women. The bumbling novice papa who could face battlefield viscera with utter equanimity but was stricken with apoplectic terror at the sight of a soiled diaper was considered a paragon of adorable masculinity. The exemplary dad was an intermittent figure—a Heroic Evanescence—disappearing every morning into a mythic world of commerce, leaving behind a vestigial nimbus of aftershave, that ghostly olfactory proxy of the ever-departing father. But no longer. Proportional caretaking and quality time are the rules du jour.

For many men, including myself, the transition from anarchic scoundrel to responsible parent is sudden and traumatic. A month or so before Gabrielle was born, I rose from the dinner table one evening, brusquely informed my wife Mercedes that I needed to split for a while, kissed her good-bye—this was all completely spur-of-the-moment—picked up a couple of buddies of mine, and off we went to this continuous ten-day concert. There was one band, The Bedouins, and they only played one song—something called "Porcelain Bisque." And the song was literally uninterrupted for ten days. (Although the song was seamless, individual band members were replaced as they became exhausted. Reserve Bedouins waiting off-stage would take over as they saw musicians beginning to falter.) On the tenth day we thought the song had ended. But it was a trick ending. A kind of false bottom. There ensued an unending series of codas. They were like encores (although it was still "Porcelain Bisque") except that sometimes it was hours before the band returned. Once, we had all left our seats and were in the parking lot walking toward our cars and we heard them start up again and we all rushed back. Later we were actually on the highway driving home and we heard on the radio that they had started again. So everyone drove back and returned to their seats. None of us knew when the song might start again, so we wore special beepers so that when another encore began we could be notified at our jobs or wherever we were and we could drive back to the arena.

Suddenly you're a father. There, in her little seat at the dinner table, wearing a fright mask of fluorescent green-pea compote and desiccated barley gruel, is little Gaby, entreating you with those big sparkling Japanese-comic-book eyes, and there's Merci, exhausted and bedraggled from a day of marathon mothering. Now, can you just get up and peremptorily announce that you're off to a Bedouins' concert? Of course not. (Well, you may make the announcement, and you may even get as far as the exit ramp for the arena, but you'll turn back, believe me.)

Unfortunately, if you simply acquiesce to this new responsibility without establishing a means to express your dark and barbaric side, you may end up unconsciously overcompensating—or "acting out"—in ways that are terribly destructive to your family and career.

I offer the example of Sloan Kerr, the award-winning architect acclaimed for his "soft houses"—habitats whose walls are composed of "intelligent" polymer gels which expand or contract in response to the aggregate body temperatures of its inhabitants, enabling the same structure to be as intimate as a library carrel one minute and as capacious as an airline terminal the next. Six months after the birth of his first child, Kerr submitted a design in competition for a new Museum of Contemporary Art in Vancouver, British Columbia. Kerr's plan called for the museum's esplanades, atria, and concourses to be sown with Misar SB-33 antipersonnel mines. Well, of course, the jury was aghast, rejecting Kerr's entry out of hand, and awarding the commission to I. M. Pei, who had submitted a somewhat more temperate design. Although Kerr claimed to have been exploring "the spatiality of vulnerability and articulations of the forbidden zone," I suspect that this was simply the case of a new and doting father psychologically maimed in the explosion of his own buried belligerence— the eruption of his "inner swaggerer."

Consider, also, a story carried recently over the AP wire about a surgeon and an anesthesiologist in Worcester, Massachusetts, who were fined $10,000 each for brawling in an operating room while their patient slept under general anesthesia. ("Dr. Chan swore at Dr. Korgaonkar, who threw a cotton-tipped prep stick at Dr. Chan . . . The two then raised their fists and scuffled briefly, at one point wrestling on the floor. A nurse monitored the anesthetized patient as the doctors fought.") Although some in the medical profession have blamed the physicians' unbecoming conduct on the influence of violent rap videos which portray "doctors" as protagonists—specifically citing hardcore rapper and producer Dr. Dre—it wouldn't surprise me if Drs. Chan and Korgaonkar were new papas who, after several months of cooing and lullabying, were simply unable to suppress their atavistic need to rumble.

Let's take a look at several easy-to-follow tips that I believe can enable you to be a decent dad whose style is irresistibly virile—predatory, wanton, ungovernable. The kind of dad who can strut through a pediatric waiting room and still feel like the reckless savage—the heavy-drinking, womanizing, expense-account cheat—that he really is, deep-down inside.

BORN A GAMBLIN' MAN

From the moment your squalling neonate passes the Apgar Test—the first rung on his or her ladder to success—you'll be deluged with advice about how to best provide for Junior's education. The world will turn avuncular with a vengeance—you'll be waylaid and buttonholed from dawn till dusk and exhorted to set up special savings and money market accounts, to purchase long-term certificates, bonds of various maturities and yields, treasury bills, etc. etc. This is all well and good, of course—investing in the kid's future is undoubtedly the wise and proper thing to do. The trouble is that the investments traditionally foisted upon new fathers are so conservative, so prudent, so safe, that they squelch the very best part of a man—that heedless, irresponsible strain of brinkmanship that can transform a pair of dice or a field-goal attempt—frozen at the apex of its flight—into an agonizing epiphany of cosmic caprice.

When looking to financially secure your child's higher education, I suggest investments with a bit more "play" to them. Lately I've been touting defaulted North Korean bank debt. According to brokers in Hong Kong, North Korean debt is trading for about 15 cents per dollar of face value. Two months ago, the debt was trading at 12 cents to the dollar. A few years back, the price was as low as 2 cents.

Pyongyang owes Western bank syndicates and foreign governments about $3 billion. Will its kooky xenophobic leaders welsh on its creditors? What's going on at that nuclear site in Yongbyon? Will U.N. saber-rattling spook Kim Jong Il into sending a million North Korean regulars, 3,500 tanks, and a blizzard of SCUDs across the DMZ? With your little cherub's tuition on the line, monitoring troop movements at the 38th parallel can be as exhilarating as a day at the track.

Sure you're a dad, but if you're a risk-taker with liquid hydrogen in those veins, investing in heavily indebted pariah states beats passbook savings any day.

WHEN TOYS AREN'T US

Buying toys, toiletries, or medical supplies for a baby can be a demoralizing experience. Nothing gelds a novice father's masculinity more efficiently than having to publicly verbalize a litany of cute product names each ending in *y* or *ies*—"Huggy Furry Yummy Chewy Cuddly Potties." And then there's the forced march home, through the inevitable gauntlet of snickering bar buddies, with you balancing a teetering pyramid of packages emblazoned with a conglomerate of ducklings, bunnies, clowns, and mermaids.

One way to mitigate some of the embarrassment is to go upscale. Several companies offer luxury versions of common infant items. They tend to be expensive, but the names, product design, and packaging are significantly more dignified. Mont Blanc recently introduced an infant rectal thermometer that I can't recommend highly enough. It's identical in size to their large Meisterstück fountain pen, and it's available in both black and bordeaux.

Even the fathers of older children encounter potential disgrace when accompanying their offspring to the toy store. The bowed heads and averted eyes of dads accompanying their swooning daughters to FAO Schwarz recently to meet actor Joey Lawrence were poignant testimony to their shame. Lawrence, heartthrob to the pubescent set thanks to his role as "Joey Russo" on the hit television series "Blossom," was appearing at the swanky Fifth Ave. toy emporium to promote a line of "Blossom" action figures, among which is, of course, the "Joey Russo" doll. Action figures are a hot ticket, according to toy industry analysts.

If you're fortunate enough to have a child who likes playing with action figures but who's too young to care what characters are represented, I recommend buying dolls that will not induce point-of-purchase nausea and that might even interest and amuse you. I bought my Gaby—who's six months old—a couple of the "This Week With David Brinkley" action figures. I've got the "Sam Donaldson" and the "Cokie Roberts" dolls. Every now and then I find myself striking up a conversation with the bendable lifelike figures, and Gaby enjoys sucking on their heads and then throwing them across the room.

I also recommend trying to depuerilize your child's toys by devising "adult" ways for you to play with them. For example, last weekend I attended a party at my agent's East Side apartment house. The fête was chockablock with celebs including Walt Disney chairman Michael Eisner, Wimbledon champ Steffi Graf, Wynonna Judd, Secretary of Defense Les Aspin, best-selling health guru Deepak Chopra, Harvard biologist and ant maven Edward O. Wilson, and Chaka Khan, among others. Unable to find a deck of cards, New York Giants linebacker and notorious high-roller Lawrence Taylor and I found a Chutes & Ladders set in our hostess's daughter's bedroom cabinet and, before an audience of hushed and appalled guests, we played a series of games with wagers in the hundreds of thousands of dollars!

INTRO TO KIDDIE LIT. 101

Put simply: It's exceedingly unattractive to sire a child who grows up to be an illiterate simp. Ergo, you must read to the kid regularly and instill a deep and abiding logophilia—any parenting how-to book will tell you as much. Where the guides go astray, particularly in light of your compensatory needs as a swaggering male, is in the recommended syllabus. Notwithstanding conventional wisdom to the contrary, you needn't read children's books to children, especially to very young children.

To illustrate my point, here's a partial list of what I've been reading to Gaby over the past month: military historian John Keegan's *The Mask of Command,* Racine's *Phèdre,* Hans Zinsser's classic *Rats, Lice and History,* and an architectural survey of Kuala Lumpur entitled *The Golden Goiter*. The secret is in the tone. Racine seems to be particularly compelling when read in a high-pitched, squeaky animated-mouse voice.

You'll feel so much better—so much more the alluring outlaw—reading the delirious confessions of a *poète maudit* to your kid than some allegory about altruistic woodchucks or punctual possums or bears who say good night to their socks. Rimbaud's *A Season in Hell* goes over like gangbusters, especially if each end-stopped line is punctuated by a loud moo or a flatulent spluttering sound. I've found that the lines "I shall detach for you these sparse hideous pages from my notebook of the damned" are most successful when recited in an ascending pitch that accelerates to a crescendo as two fingers scamper from the child's tippy-toes to her chin. This, of course, can be repeated ad infinitum with no discernable diminution of effect.

It's almost impossible to predict which selections will prove most entertaining to your little one. A passage from Edmund White's new biography of Jean Genet describing how one night Genet took too many Nembutals and danced in a pink negligée for a roomful of Black Panthers induces, in Gaby, uncontrollable hysterics that invariably culminate in hiccups. (Please note that reactions to this passage may vary from child to child.)

THE GIFT THAT KEEPS ON GIVING

The gifted child is a particularly dapper addition to your lifestyle. To my taste, nothing garnishes a man's virility, nothing expresses the elegance of his genetic matrix, quite like his very own prodigy.

Unfortunately, the spate of current magazines and books devoted to the subject will be of little use in determining whether your pride and joy is the genuine article. The criteria for a gifted child have become ludicrously slack. Here are several corroborating attributes from an article entitled "Is Your Child Gifted" that appeared recently in *American Baby* magazine: Holds a small object between fingers and thumb (before six months); points to at least one named body part (before 12 months); asks "why" or "how come" (before 24 months).

Please.

We, as a society, have obviously allowed our pathological belief in entitlement to degrade even the standards for our own children's precocity.

Can your son or daughter: Move a small object telekinetically (before six months); point to at least one named endocrine gland (before 12 months); ask "why does evil exist if God is good and omnipotent?" (before 24 months)?

If you can respond affirmatively to any of *these* questions—then, maybe, we can start talking *gifted*.

One note of caution: A gifted child's gift is not always a pretty one. Here's a conversation I overheard recently in the playground of the Genesis Institute, a gifted-children elementary school in Grofton Hill, New Jersey. See if you can guess which of the interlocutors is the eight-year-old and which are the adults:

> A: The inability of Charlene Gail Heffner to coexist amicably with her adoptive mother, tobacco heiress Doris Duke, when she stood to inherit an estate worth over one billion dollars strikes me as a stunning example of strategic ineptitude. Notwith-

standing the uniquely seamy circumstances of their relationship, it's a cautionary tale for anyone with a rich parent.

B: I hear you. I mean, say your dad's the Sultan of Brunei—y'know, the guy who recently gave a $150,000 tip to a hotel chambermaid for bringing him a pumice stone. So there you are in your room in one of the summer chateaus and you're blasting your Smashing Pumpkins, and Dad—the Sultan—says turn it down and you're all ready to launch into one of your bombastic, vituperative adolescent tirades about not having asked to be born and what a dickhead your father is and all that—well, stop, take a deep breath, and think for a minute. If you play your cards right and act the dutiful son and *suffer* along with the bathysphere and the Indy-car driving lessons and the takeout from Bouley—when the Sultan kicks, you're a multibillionaire, dude. Then you can *buy* the goddamn Smashing Pumpkins, imprison them in the catacombs of your Black Sea castle, and make them play or do whatever you want them to do—whenever you want them to do it. Foresight and forbearance—that's key.

C: Definitely. I've been reading the Tibetan Book of the Dead and there's this stage called the "Bardo of Dying"—that's right before you croak and go off into the "Luminous Bardo of Dharmata"—well, that's when you gotta get to them if you're not in the will. Even if you were a real asshole to them and they cut you out completely—no inheritance, no trust fund, no annuity, zilch—there's still time, there's this Bardo of Opportunity. But you have to have the skills. The Tibetans have been studying this stuff for thousands of years.

Give up? Well, surprise. Each of these charming *dramatis personae* is an eight-year-old Genesis Institute student. And the gift that genetic serendipity has bestowed upon them is a chilling Machiavellianism and remorseless cunning that would make even the most ruthless grifter blanch.

LONE WOLF AND CUB

All men need their R and R, but new fathers intent on maintaining a finely honed, aggressive manhood have special recreational requirements. I consider a regimen of high-risk sports almost mandatory. But how do you balance this need for perilous pastimes with the obligation to spend quality time with your infant? Simple: Take the little tyke along!

Mountain climbing has become an increasingly popular means for fathers and their babies to share the thrill of physical conquest. Manufacturers of alpine equipment now offer specially designed oxygen canisters that accommodate an infant's pulmonary needs in thin air. Purists, though, like legendary mountaineer Reinhold Messner, consider the use of such conveniences "cheating." Messner recently scaled Kangchenjunga, a 28,169-foot peak on the border of India and Nepal, with his seven-month-old son Hellmut—and without supplemental oxygen *or* fixed guide-ropes for Hellmut's stroller.

If you prefer to recreate with your infant at ground level, I suggest marathon running. I think you'll enjoy the challenge of scampering 26 miles with the little one in your arms. (Backpack infant-carriers, though available, are also frowned upon by roadrunning purists.) Don't be discouraged from participating by the fact that your baby is nursing. Most marathon sponsors provide lactating women at stations along the race course who offer out-stretched bottles of warm breast milk.

For the sheer adrenaline rush, I, personally, don't think anything quite matches drag racing. For those few ecstatic seconds of screaming engines and blurred asphalt, it all seems to make sense—birth, death, quantum mechanics, black holes, enlargement of the prostate, alimony . . . for that instant, it all seems woven into some gorgeous and divine tapestry.

Beyond its contemplative benefits, drag racing is a won-derful sport in which to participate with your infant. Babies find the gentle motion of accelerating G-forces reminiscent of motion within Mommy's womb. There's a wide range of helmets and Kevlar accessories available for infants. It's very important to select the proper drag-racing car seat for your child. There are two main types: the in-fant drag-racing car seat which faces backward and the toddler seat, which is front-facing. Safety seats employ a variety of restraint mechanisms, although I prefer the one-latch harness—it makes it easier to unfasten the baby once your dragster's chute has opened. Always look for the Ju-venile Drag-Racing Products Manufacturers Association (JDRPMA) certification seal.

Japanese comic artists Kazuo Koike and Goseki Kojima have provided us with perhaps the most potent icon of the virile father and his child: outlaw samurai and assassin, Itto Ogami, who slashes his way across feudal Japan ac-companied by his infant son, Daigoro, who rides in a wooden baby cart equipped with spears, spring blades, and smoke bombs. Together, they are known as "Lone Wolf and Cub."

One afternoon Gaby and I were gazing up at the poster of Lone Wolf and Cub that looms above my writing desk, when Gaby, as is her wont, whacked me in the face with the back of her lolling head. The talismanic image of the glowering samurai and his impassive son combined with the sensation of blood flowing from my nostrils gave me a sudden inspiration: Infant As Martial Arts Weapon. There I was, incapacitated with pain, blood gushing from my nose, and there was Gaby, unscathed, chortling with glee. It was inconceivable to me, though, that an idea this perfect hadn't been considered previously by someone, somewhere, so I did some research at the local library. Sure enough, it turns out that in the 13th century on a small island near Okinawa, the indigenous population had developed just such a fighting technique.

Apparently, a brutal occupying force had forbidden the native inhabitants to possess weapons. Needing some means to fight their oppressors, a secret society of monks first experimented with using their elderly as weapons, but they turned out to be too brittle. Infants, considerably more supple, were tried next and with great success. (See the *Tao Te Ching* for the superiority of "the supple" over "the brittle.") Without suffering the slightest injury or discomfort, the infant was able to inflict great pain on an opponent.

A comprehensive martial art was developed in which the infant's body is wielded as a kind of deluxe nunchaku. Gripped at the ankles and swung, the infant's head becomes a devastating bludgeon. Swung with arms outstretched and fingers splayed, the infant's razor-sharp nails rake the face of an attacker with gruesome stopping power. More esoteric techniques include *jee xua ji* ("cheesing")—this technique, only practiced by the most adept masters, actually utilizes an infant's projectile regurgitation of milk to blind an assailant.

If you're considering taking up this sport—which is great fun for father *and* child—don't try teaching yourself at home, enroll in a school. I was sparring with my upstairs neighbor, who has a little girl a month or so younger than Gaby, and I didn't grip Gab's ankle correctly, and I ended up breaking the third metacarpal bone in my right hand. And, remember, when choosing a school, only consider those which employ certified instructors.

NOW IT'S YOUR TURN

As I make the final adjustments on Gaby's sidecar—we're about to attempt a motorcycle jump over the thirty-story glass pyramid at the new Luxor casino in Las Vegas, the first motorcycle jump of its kind *ever* attempted conjointly with a six-month-old—I am filled with excitement for you as you begin *your* mission.

Learn and incorporate my simple methods at your own individual pace. As you become proficient with each tool, add it to your utility belt. When you're finished with my course, you'll be fully equipped to swagger through any Chuck E. Cheese in America. To history's honorifics of virility—"brigand," "defiler," "conquistador," "warlord"—you'll be able to add, with unalloyed pride: "Dad."

I was recently conference-called by a threesome of Chicago entrepreneurs who wanted to know if I'd be interested in writing video scripts for their company. Although my verbal pledge of confidentiality probably isn't worth squat in a court of law, it wouldn't be "nice" to divulge details of their enterprise. Let's just say that the project involved producing educational videos for kids which would be shown in schools, and that there was an oblique commercial component for corporate sponsors.

Now, I've been out of the advertising business for some six years. But I've never quite gotten it out of my system—that charged office milieu that requires agile, lightning-quick shifts from ruthless predation to abject, butt-slobbering sycophancy; those epiphanic moments when you realize that yes! yes! shameless pandering *is* a craft, and enraptured, you wring a gorgeous mercenary music from your keyboard of market-researched hot buttons like some Faustian lunatic flailing at his pipe organ in some sulfurous catacomb!

So I said OK, I'll take a meeting.

I meet with these guys and right off the bat I can see that they're mice and not men (from a business perspective), and that this project is going absolutely nowhere. And I'm evincing skepticism all over the place: sighing, drumming my fingers on the conference table, cracking my neck, working my cuticles with an orange stick, blowing bubbles in my coffee . . .

"What's wrong?" says one finally. "You don't look too enthusiastic."

"The bottom line here is getting a plug for your sponsors' products, right? Well, this whole vehicle is too subtle, too namby pamby. How are these kids going to remember the products when you're being so goddamn diffident?"

"First of all, Mark, the bottom line here is education."

I rolled my eyes and blew a major bubble cluster in the espresso.

"Second of all, we have to be very circumspect about the insertion of advertising into the curriculum. Look at the criticism Whittle got for airing commercials with their educational programming. Look at the flak Mirage Resorts just got for that kiddie infomercial 'Treasure Island.'"

"They're holding high school classes at the Mall of America in Minneapolis for Christ's sake. School at the mall! What are you guys worried about?"

"I just think you have to be very careful about mixing education and commercialism."

"Crap. Commercialism is all a lot of kids have to hang

on to anymore. Look, I've got an idea for you guys that's not only a pedagogical godsend but will also give your sponsors some high-profile name recognition. You know how product placement in movies has become such a big business? Like L'Oréal pays Tristar a fee and in some scene where Demi Moore is about to Matahari the nuts off some Eurotrash narcoterrorist, the camera pans to her dressing table and lingers on a jar of Plénitude Hydra-Renewal cream for a couple of seconds. Well, how about product placement in literature textbooks?"

"You mean like put ad inserts in a book of Shakespeare plays?"

"Not ads. I'm talking about something much more sophisticated. I'm talking about interpolating product names into the text itself. So that kids come across a sponsor's product as if it were part of the original work. Kids love product names and logos—just look at the clothes they wear. So we'd actually be enhancing the literature so that *maybe* they read the stuff, and we'd be reinforcing brand recognition every time they get an English assignment."

They grimace at me dyspeptically. "Aren't children going to take umbrage at being issued adulterated textbooks?"

"You think they'll even know? There's the present and then there's this dumpster of undifferentiated synchronic trivia called 'history.' Ask a kid today which happened first, the Peloponnesian Wars or the Korean War—no clue, I assure you. Eyes glazed, drool down the chin, total blank. We're talking about people who wouldn't know Ernie Kovacs from Sandy Koufax, for Christ's sake. Look, you mentioned Shakespeare before . . ."

I pull a textbook out of my briefcase.

". . . let me show you what I'm talking about. Here's

Antony and Cleopatra. I'll just open this up randomly to show you how easy this can be . . . OK, here . . . oh, this is just *too* easy—here's this character Enobarbus speaking: 'The city cast / Her people out upon her; and Antony / Enthroned i'th' market place, did sit alone, / Whistling to th' air; which, but for vacancy, / Had gone to gaze on Cleopatra too, / And made a gap in nature.' "

I make two fast proofreader's marks in the text and hand it to them. "Voilà. Now, in *our* version those last two lines read: 'Had gone to gaze on Cleopatra too, / And made *The Gap* in nature.' Pretty amazing, huh? And the demographics are perfect for Gap Inc.—junior high, high school, college."

Three blank stares.

I reach back into my briefcase.

"Willa Cather. *My Antonia.* A perennial favorite of English teachers everywhere. Let's just open her up here . . . OK . . . They're talking about some guy, Mr. Shimerda: 'His face had a look of weariness and pleasure, like that of sick people when they feel relief from pain. Grandmother insisted on his drinking a glass of Virginia apple-brandy after his long walk in the cold . . . ' "

I make several flourishes with my blue pen and presto: " 'His face had a look of weariness and pleasure, like that of sick people when they feel relief from pain. Grandmother insisted on his drinking a *40-oz. bottle of St. Ides malt liquor* after his long walk in the cold . . . '

"It's that easy, gentlemen. Seamless product insertions percolating into the minds of our young scholars. And it works with any genre. You guys familiar with the Japanese haiku poet Bashō? Well, this is a little tricky because you gotta maintain the right syllable count . . . OK, listen to this: 'Seven sights were veiled / In mist—then I heard / Mii Temple's bell.' How about something like: 'Seven sights were veiled / In mist—then I heard / *The Taco Bell.*' Not bad, huh? And it scans!"

After considerable paper shuffling and throat clearing, the trio demurs in a gutless arpeggio.

"Mark, I don't think this is the direction we really had in mind."

"I'm afraid it's a little aggressive for me."

"Might spook the sponsors."

"Spook the sponsors?" I say, packing up my things. "Listen, when you boys grow up and decide that you want to do some *real* advertising, give me a call. Until then . . . I'm outa here."

On the way home from the airport, I stop at Cosmo's Bakery in Hoboken for a cup of coffee and something sweet and gooey. Cosmo has just taken a tray of jelly doughnuts from the oven.

"Mark, how ya doin'?"

"Not bad, Cosmo."

"What are you workin' on?"

"I'm writing this 'Shouts and Murmurs' piece for *The New Yorker* about companies inserting their products' names into literature textbooks for school kids."

"The companies have to pay, right? It's like they do in movies."

"Exactly, Coz."

"Hey, what would it cost me to get my bakery mentioned in the piece?"

"In the 'Shouts and Murmurs' piece?"

"Yeah, what would it cost me?"

"Jeez, I don't know, Coz. Let me think . . . maybe $500 for a mention."

He pulls a thick money roll out of his pocket and peels off five crisp C-notes, each emblazoned with a big flour thumbprint.

I take the cash. "Consider it done, Cosmo."

"How much to mention I got zeppoles every Saturday?"

"Jeez, Coz, c'mon . . . did I come in here selling space?"

He peels off another five Franklins.

I take the money. "Done," I say.

"Mark, don't just stick it in real obvious. Make it part of the flow, you know what I'm sayin'?"

"Seamless, Cosmo, seamless. I'm a professional."

I snatch a jelly doughnut from the tray and exit through a jingling door into frigid air and blinding sunlight. My eyes glaze. A dollop of warm jelly oozes down my chin. I feel good.

Spook the sponsors. What a crock.

o h ,
brother

Aaron and Joshua Zeichner are twin brothers charged with first-degree murder in the artillery, grenade, and submachine gun killings of their parents, Sam and Adele. Aaron and Joshua, twenty-three years old, are being defended by the impassioned, histrionic, tactically virtuosic attorney Susannah Levine. Levine has argued that her clients, who admit to the killings, were induced by irrational fears into believing, mistakenly but honestly, that their parents were about to kill them. Mounting a defense that featured a cavalcade of expert witnesses and culminated in the riveting and lurid testimony of the brothers themselves, Levine has methodically constructed the theory that even though they were not at the moment of the killing under direct threat, the Zeichner twins killed their father and mother out of fear for their own lives. Levine has implored the jury to apply the concept of "imperfect self-defense" and render a verdict of voluntary manslaughter—a verdict that would save the twins from the electric chair and might result in prison terms of only several years.

But here all similarities to the Los Angeles trial of Erik and Lyle Menendez end.

Unlike the Menendez boys and their attorney, Leslie Abramson, who claim that a history of abuse made the brothers fear that their parents were about to kill them, Levine and the Zeichner twins maintain that, conversely, it was a history of loving, exemplary parenting that drove the boys to kill their mom and dad in self-defense.

It's unfortunate that the Menendez trial—set amid the wealth, privilege, and glitter of Beverly Hills, showcased by daily coverage on Court T.V., decocted for the rabble each morning in indignant tabloid bold and expatiated upon by an all-star squad of belletrists wringing Racinian drama from the ergonomic keyboards of their Power-Books—has all but eclipsed the Zeichner case. Trent Oaks—where Sam and Adele Zeichner were slaughtered in a twenty-minute barrage of howitzer shells, rocket-propelled grenades, and expanding 9-mm Luger combat rounds as they sat in their den working on Aaron's University of Pennsylvania application essay—is no Beverly Hills. It's a rather unremarkable middle- to upper-class suburb whose shopping mall and high school soccer team are its main sources of pride and distinction.

No cable channels, no tabloids, no Dominick Dunnes have found their way to the modest, stucco, Tudor-style Trent Oaks County Administration Building. In fact, the gallery is often empty except for family members, a prospective witness or two, and me. (I'm covering the

Zeichner trial for the German magazine *Der Gummiknüppel*.) The disparity in media attention is particularly regrettable because the Zeichner case provides an even more illuminating anatomy of the "imperfect self-defense" theory—and its implications for our society—than does the Menendez trial.

Here we have no abusive miserable childhoods, no tyrannical father, no disturbed mother. We have, to the contrary, a pampered Edenic youth. We have Sam Zeichner, a father who undergoes rotator-cuff surgery just so he can pitch batting practice to his eight-year-old son, Aaron, an uncoordinated, astigmatic child dying to make his local Little League team. Sam Zeichner, a father who spends a month of weeknights and weekends sculpting a topographical battlefield map of Waterloo out of marzipan for little Joshua, a Napoleonic War buff with a bulimic craving for molded almond paste. And we have Adele Zeichner—vivacious, gregarious, resourceful, indulgent Adele Zeichner—who, determined to give her children every possible advantage, commuted to work with Walkman earphones splayed against her pregnant belly so that Aaron and Joshua could listen—in utero—to Telly Savalas reading Pindar's Epinician Odes in ancient Greek. Adele Zeichner, racking her brain each and every morning to come up with a new sandwich for her boys to take to school. From Fluffernutters and clotted cream on date-nut bread to shaved Kobe beef on crustless challah and tripe with melted Stilton on focaccia—in twelve years of public education the Zeichner twins never found the same sandwich in their lunch boxes. (A logistics expert testifying for the defense estimated that Adele Zeichner prepared more than 1,920 unique sandwiches for her boys.)

Photographs of the boys' bedroom reveal children who

wanted for nothing: there were large-screen televisions, CD-ROM computers, cellular phones, vintage Coke machines, souvlaki rotisseries, etc. Birthdays were celebrated with Hammacher Schlemmer catalog binges, backstage passes for Def Leppard, Super Bowl box seats on the fifty-yard line, treks through the Ecuadorean rain forest. How many kids do you know who received blowguns, curare-tipped darts, and a three-layer manioc birthday cake from hallucinogen-addled Jivaro headhunters for their tenth birthday?

But this wasn't simply a case of parents obliviously lavishing material objects on their children. There was nurturing and understanding and support at every juncture of their upbringing. There were special tutors if the boys had trouble with algebra, sports psychologists when they faltered in gym class. When the time came for those inevitable adolescent experiments, be it Satanism or transvestism, Mom and Dad were right there to facilitate these difficult rites of passage—Sam rummaging through his cartons of college books for a volume of Aleister Crowley, Adele loaning Josh a velvet-piped, silk chiffon Carolina Herrera for a cruise through the mall. Never was a hand raised in anger, never was a sarcastic or deprecating remark directed at those boys. Often neighbors would notice lights in the master bedroom burning deep into the night as Sam and Adele sat and listened patiently to their sons' teenage tribulations, determined to treat them respectfully, without carping or condescension.

And with each caring gesture, Aaron and Joshua grew increasingly certain that their parents were going to kill them. The more sympathetic and generous Sam and Adele were, the more fearful their sons became that their parents were about to snap. Or so Susannah Levine would have us believe.

As argued by their attorney, and according to their own sworn testimony, the Zeichner twins had become inculcated by television with the belief that normal parents are confrontational, contemptuous, and abusive. Consequently, they perceived their parents' gentle and empathic behavior as "bizarre," "frightening," and, ultimately, "a grave threat."

Addressing the jury in her opening remarks, and frequently punctuating the idea by banging her head against a stanchion near the jury box, Levine asked: "How many made-for-television movies, how many celebrity confessions, how many episodes of '60 Minutes' and '48 Hours' and '20/20' and 'Prime Time Live' and 'Eye to Eye with Connie Chung' did these boys have to watch before they became convinced that normal parenting is abusive, that the relationship between a parent and a child is violently adversarial—and that their parents, Sam and Adele Zeichner, were *not normal,* that something was terribly, terribly odd about the way their parents were treating them? In Aaron and Joshua's minds, their parents were either consciously dissimulating—in other words, perpetrating some sort of evil ruse to lull the boys into a false sense of security—or they were unconsciously repressing their inner desires to kill their children. To Aaron and Joshua, each new gift and each successive gesture of compassion brought them one step closer to what they called 'the breaking point.' "

Under direct examination, Joshua discussed the time he and his brother first realized their parents were spinning dangerously out of control.

LEVINE: Was there a time when you and Aaron were *not* scared of your parents?

JOSHUA: When we were very young, we thought that the way our parents behaved was normal. We just figured that's how every family was—until we became aware of how other parents treated their kids.

LEVINE: You became aware of this from watching television?

JOSHUA: From TV and from other kids.

LEVINE: Was there one incident in particular—a dinner?

JOSHUA: Yeah. I'd been bugging Mom for a week or so to make lobster in black bean sauce, which was one of my favorite things. So this one day Mom decided to make it for me and she told me to invite a friend. And as soon as she came home from work that afternoon, she started cooking. And it's a pretty involved meal because she makes all these side dishes and everything so it was taking a really long time and me and Aaron and our friend Sean, who was eating over, we got really hungry, so we went to Wendy's and we just stuffed ourselves. And then when we got home, we saw that Mom had set this beautiful table and she looked really tired but she was sort of beaming because she knew how much I loved what she'd made. Anyway, we all sat down, and me and Aaron and Sean couldn't eat a single bite we were so stuffed. And we had to tell my parents that we'd just gone out to Wendy's because we hadn't felt like waiting.

LEVINE: And what did your parents say?

JOSHUA: They said they understood that sometimes when you're very hungry, your stomach gets the better of you, and Mom said don't worry about missing out on the meal, that she'd make lobster in black bean sauce sandwiches for us to take to school tomorrow.

And they said it was silly for us just to sit there at the table—why didn't we go off and play and have a good time.

LEVINE: When you were all off by yourselves that night, do you remember what your friend said?

JOSHUA: He said that our parents were really, really weird. He said that if he'd done what we'd done his parents would have beaten him within an inch of his life. He was just astonished and I think appalled at how our parents reacted.

LEVINE: Do you remember how you and Aaron felt that night?

JOSHUA: Very, very scared.

LEVINE: Joshua, I want to leap ahead now from this first night of fear to your final, culminating night of fear. On the night after your high school graduation, did your parents present you and Aaron with graduation gifts?

JOSHUA: Yes. Our parents gave each of us a brand-new Infiniti J30.

LEVINE: And do you remember how you felt that night?

JOSHUA: We were absolutely *terrified*. We felt that this was the final straw. And we knew that unless we did something first we were goners.

LEVINE: When you say "the final straw" and "goners," what do you mean?

JOSHUA: That they were going to kill us.

LEVINE: And by "doing something first," what did you mean?

JOSHUA: A preemptive strike.

The "preemptive strike" that Joshua Zeichner referred to in his testimony will certainly go down in history as one of the most brutal assaults in the annals of parricide.

★ ★ ★

The boys positioned a 105-mm howitzer on a small hill several blocks from the Zeichner residence. Using infrared and night-scope equipment, they launched a fusillade of artillery rounds on their home. Scores of spent brass casings found by police offer grim testimony to the relentless salvos. Following the howitzer barrage, the twins drove one of the new Infiniti J30s back to the house. From the trunk of the car, they removed a Soviet-made RPG—an infantry-held, antitank, rocket grenade launcher—a Heckler & Koch MP5SD3 9-mm submachine gun and a Glock twenty-round 9-mm semiautomatic pistol. Aaron, wearing IL-7 Mini-Laser IR illuminator goggles attached to a Kevlar infantry ballistic helmet, knelt on the front lawn and fired a dozen of the cone-shaped, armor-piercing, rocket-propelled grenades into the den where his parents had been working. The boys then clambered through the den window and raked the room with 9-mm submachine gun fire.

Aaron offered details of the assault when he testified under direct examination:

> LEVINE: Do you know what your parents were doing in the den?
> AARON: They were writing Josh's essay for Penn.
> LEVINE: Why were they writing it? Why hadn't Josh written his own essay?
> AARON: Josh had just thrown together this really awful essay. You couldn't even call it an "essay," it was just this piece of garbage he scrawled down in two minutes and he showed it to our parents and they said, "Dear, why don't you work on this a little more and see if you can refine some of the interesting thoughts

you sketched out here" or something like that. And it was due the next day. But Josh didn't want to work on it that night.

LEVINE: Can you recall why not?

AARON: I think because "Baywatch" was on—that was one of our favorite shows.

LEVINE: So when your parents asked Josh to rewrite his essay and Josh said no because it conflicted with your plans to view "Baywatch," how did your parents react?

AARON: They said something like "Josh, you've been under a lot of stress lately, why don't you enjoy your program with your brother and we'll write the essay for you."

LEVINE: How did that make you feel?

AARON: Absolutely terrified. We were sure at that point that our parents were planning to kill us.

LEVINE: Can you explain to the court why you thought that?

AARON: We just thought it was like the final stage in their whole passive-aggressive approach to us— this whole being-so-super-nice-to-us thing had to flip into the really hostile thing sooner or later, and we decided that night that it was going to happen.

LEVINE: How many artillery shells hit the section of the house where your parents were working?

AARON: I think we got three or four direct hits.

LEVINE: Then you two went in?

AARON: No. First I fired a couple of the grenades into the den.

LEVINE: You were the first to enter the den?

AARON: Yes.

LEVINE: Was your father alive?

AARON: No.

LEVINE: And your mom?

AARON: She was alive—barely.

LEVINE: Aaron, how many rounds does a Heckler & Koch 9-mm submachine gun magazine hold?

AARON: Thirty-two.

LEVINE: And how many magazines did you and your brother fire?

AARON: I think we went through about eight clips.

LEVINE: And then what happened?

AARON: We ran out of ammunition—and Mom was still alive. So we decided to go to the store and buy more, but we didn't have any money.

LEVINE: What did you do then?

AARON: I asked Mom for money.

LEVINE: And what did she say?

AARON: She said to get her wallet out of her pocketbook and take what we needed.

LEVINE: And when you returned home with fresh ammunition, what was your mother doing? Was she trying to get out of the room?

AARON: No, she was trying to finish the essay.

LEVINE: Your honor, I have no further questions for the witness at this time.

Susannah Levine is one of several controversial defense lawyers, both lauded and vilified by their colleagues, who bring the full weight of their notoriety to bear on every case they try.

National Association of Defense Attorneys President Blair Potters, introducing Levine at a recent NADA junket in Cozumel, Mexico, said: "Imagine a Mayan architect-priestess who transforms a rank, uninhabitable tract of jungle into an intricate maze of aqueducts, sluices, and sewers whose mathematical and astrological symbology is only apprehensible when viewed from an airplane, and you'll have some idea of the scope of Susannah Levine's accomplishment in constructing cogent, elegant defenses out of the tangled mental landscapes of her clients."

Of all Levine's courtroom maneuvers and pyrotechnics, none provokes as much debate and invective as her zealous advocacy of the imperfect self-defense theory—the theory that a person, although not actually under attack, but who *believes* that he or she *will* be killed, can claim self-defense as a mitigating and even exculpatory motive in the commission of a homicide.

Walter M. Elkin, a former prosecutor and now a law professor at F.I.T. in New York, has written a series of op-ed pieces denouncing the theory as "nihilistic," and criticizing Levine for what he calls "pernicious and self-serving evangelism."

"If we allow people to murder each other as a result of perceived threats of hypothetical menace, our communities will quickly disintegrate into atomized, internecine war zones," Elkin said. "We will become a nation of 250 million belligerent tribes of one."

Levine is unapologetic. "My responsibility is to defend my clients to the very best of my ability. If I'm shrill or monomaniacal, it's because I care so deeply about them— they're decent people who've been caught in the undertow of a paradoxical culture, and they're thrashing in the dark to stay alive.

"The Cold War didn't end, it devolved from the geostrategic to the interpersonal. Imperfect self-defense is just a legal byproduct of the preemptive first-strike doctrine that now governs our behavior on the streets and in our bedrooms. We need to move toward an interpersonal version of MAD—mutually assured destruction. If each of us is sufficiently armed and booby-trapped to ensure massive reciprocal damage to everyone else, we might be deterred from murdering one another. There will be a kind of pandemic stalemate, and then you won't need people like me ranting in courtrooms, banging our heads, and spitting up in the name of justice."

On completion of the Zeichner case, Levine is off to Minneapolis, where she's defending a young woman who, believing that her parents thought she was going to kill them, deduced that they were going to preemptively kill her, so she killed them first—in other words, preempting an erroneously anticipated preemption.

"This should be a wild one," Levine enthused. "We're dealing with infinitely reflecting mirror images of fear—Chinese boxes of paranoia within boxes of paranoia."

Late one afternoon—the Zeichner case had just gone to the jury—I watched Levine toss her briefcase into a factory-fresh, jade-green Infiniti J30 parked in front of the Trent Oaks County Administration Building. She saw me scrutinizing the car.

"It's my retainer," she shrugged.

"Is that Aaron's or Joshua's?" I asked.

"Aaron's. I actually like Josh's better—it's red—but they impounded it as evidence."

I laughed.

"Seriously," she said, "if you ever kill your parents . . ."

She handed me her card.

"Listen, my parents were pretty wonderful," I said, "but they were no Sam and Adele Zeichner!"

She shook her head ominously. "They were probably

much better than even you know. You probably don't even remember the *really* good things they did to you. It could take years of therapy before it all comes out."

She revved the engine and vanished in a plume of exhaust.

The streets were empty thanks to the draconian provisions of a newly enacted curfew that prohibited armed teenagers from congregating in public after 3 P.M. The crepuscular sky was a pousse-café of azure, rose, and vermillion.

I popped a cassette into my Walkman, and listened as Telly Savalas intoned Pindar's twelfth Olympian ode:

Hai ge men andrôn
poll' anô, ta d' au katô
pseudê metamônia tamnoisai kulindont' elpides

"Men's hopes, in endless undulation, soar and plummet, borne on falsehoods, that heave and tumble, in the wind."

m y   d i

April 11, 1994

FROM: Jeanette Walls, Esquire Magazine

Dear Sir:

This summer, writer Peter Lefcourt is coming out
with a book, DI AND I, in which he imagines going
on a date with Princess Diana.

We thought it would be fun to ask some of the
world's best-known men: If you were eligible and you
were taking out Princess Diana, what would you do?
Where would you go? Or what would you talk?

We would love it if you would participate in this.
Responses can be brief (a sentence or two would be
fine, but can be longer if you like) and can be phoned
in to me at (212)555-4291 or faxed to (212)555-0251.
We're planning to run the article in the June issue, so
we need replies by the 20th of April. Thanks so much
for your help on this.

Sincerely,
Jeanette Walls
Contributing Editor,
Esquire Magazine

LEYNER

You know, S. I. Newhouse's father dated my grand-mother Harriet.

PRINCESS DI

How lovely.

LEYNER

Yeah . . . they were teenagers. This must have been, oh, sixty, seventy years ago. She was from Jersey City, he was from Bayonne.

PRINCESS DI

Bayonne? In 1808, at Bayonne, Napoleon forced Charles IV and Ferdinand VII of Spain to abdicate. At the end of the Peninsula War, Bayonne successfully resisted a British siege. Bayonne gives its name to the bayonet, invented there in the seventeenth century. Weird, that I still remember all that bloody stuff . . .

LEYNER

That's Bayonne, France, babe. I'm talking about Bayonne, New Jersey.

PRINCESS DI

I've never been to Bayonne, New Jersey, I don't think.

LEYNER

Maybe later we'll go . . .

Later

PRINCESS DI

You have very soft skin for a man.

LEYNER

I do all my own chemabrasions, and I make my own fortifying nourishing cremes and hydro-replenishing treatments . . . I'm quite handy with the chemicals.

PRINCESS DI

Oh?

LEYNER

And I'm a bit of an amateur dermatologist.

PRINCESS DI

A hobby, then?

LEYNER

Do you see this over here?

PRINCESS DI

What?

LEYNER

Wait . . . it's too dark. Let me get that uh . . . damn it, I can't reach the—

PRINCESS DI

Should I get up?

LEYNER

No no no! This is perfect. Please—

PRINCESS DI

Yes, it is quite . . . comfortable. Quite nice.

LEYNER

Could you just reach up and turn on that light right there.

PRINCESS DI

This one here?

LEYNER

Yeah . . . thanks. OK, do you see where I'm pointing, here on my calf? I used to have a mole—which is actually a category of *nevus*—right here. I excised it myself. Look—not the slightest trace of a scar. Clean as a whistle.

PRINCESS DI

Extraordinary. One would never suspect you had any category of nevus there, never! Would it be a terrible imposition to ask you to take a look at something?

LEYNER

Not at all. It would be an honor and a treat.

PRINCESS DI

OK. If I could just . . . could you lift yourself up a little so I could get my arm out from under . . . thanks. OK, do you see this right here? Do you know what that is?

LEYNER

That, if I'm not mistaken, is also a category of nevus called a *hemangioma*. And this particular sort of hemangioma is commonly known as a *strawberry mark*.

PRINCESS DI

Do you think it needs to come off?

LEYNER

Absolutely not. First of all, it's quite harmless . . . and secondly, it's really quite adorable!

PRINCESS DI

You're really too kind. Your wife is a very fortunate woman.

LEYNER

She's fabulous. Would you like to see a photograph of her and my daughter?

PRINCESS DI

Why, yes, yes I would.

LEYNER

OK . . . if you could just roll over a bit so I could reach my wallet . . . OK, there we go. Now, this is Merci—her real name is Mercedes. She's from Ecuador. And that's Gabrielle, who's almost 10 months old now.

PRINCESS DI

What a precious little girl. And your wife is stunning—like some sort of Incan . . . supermodel! What is this we're drinking, by the way?

LEYNER

It's my own invention, actually. It's equal parts of Yoo-Hoo and vodka with half a crushed Valium sprinkled on top. There are any number of variations. You can use chocolate milk—Bosco, Nestle's Quik, Ovaltine, whatever—I just happen to prefer the taste of Yoo-Hoo, and it's pre-made, which I find more convenient. And you don't have to use vodka—you can go with gin, a light rum, tequila, grain alcohol, whatever suits your taste. And if you don't like the Valium, you can experiment with all sorts of toppings—Librium works nicely, Miltown, some people prefer half a Percodan—you can be creative.

PRINCESS DI

Ummmmm . . . it's very smooth.

LEYNER

I'm a little buzzed. How about you?

PRINCESS DI

To be terribly terribly honest with you, I feel awfully good. Have you given it a name?

LEYNER

Soma.

PRINCESS DI

Ah . . . from Huxley.

LEYNER

You're a reader?

PRINCESS DI

Used to be, I'm afraid. Lately I've grown rather addicted to the telly. It's probably a bit of reaction to my life with Charles. We never watched television. Oh, never. Nights we'd sit there in this huge room, me on one side reading some edifying tome that mum-in-law had chosen for me, and Charles all the way on the other side with his custom-made extra-large Walkman earphones on, listening to his Welsh language instructional tapes—y'know he was keen on speaking Welsh whenever he had to appear in Wales on royal business. And y'know how loud people are when they sing along with music on the Walkman? Well, there we'd be sitting in utter and complete silence for great stretches of time, and suddenly from the other side of the room, there'd be this volcanic belch of Welsh pronoun declension. And then another twenty minutes of bloody nothing. God, it was boring! Give me some decent pabulum on the telly any day.

LEYNER

What's your favorite show?

PRINCESS DI

"Matlock."

LEYNER

You're kidding!?

PRINCESS DI

Why?

LEYNER

That's mine too. That's amazing.

PRINCESS DI

It's pretty roomy back here. What kind of car is this?

LEYNER

It's a Nissan Altima.

PRINCESS DI

It's quite . . . oh dear, I've gone and spilled my Soma all over little Gabrielle's car seat! Oh I'm such an oaf! Charles was forever telling me what a spastic I was, and he was right! I'm so sorry . . .

LEYNER

Don't worry about it.

PRINCESS DI

Oh, I'm so terribly sorry.

LEYNER

Really, don't worry about it. There's plenty more where that came from.

PRINCESS DI

You're an awfully good sport.

LEYNER

Here, let me freshen that up for you. There we go. To "Matlock."

PRINCESS DI

To "Matlock" . . . and us.

LEYNER

To us.